The Life and Romances of Mrs. Eliza Haywood

The Life and Romances of Mrs. Eliza Haywood

George Whicher

MINT EDITIONS

The Life and Romances of Mrs. Eliza Haywood was first published in 1915.

This edition published by Mint Editions 2021.

ISBN 9781513291604 | E-ISBN 9781513294452

Published by Mint Editions®

MINT
EDITIONS

minteditionbooks.com

Publishing Director: Jennifer Newens
Design & Production: Rachel Lopez Metzger
Project Manager: Micaela Clark
Typesetting: Westchester Publishing Services

Contents

I

Eliza Haywood's Life

Autobiography was almost the only form of writing not attempted by Eliza Haywood in the course of her long career as an adventuress in letters. Unlike Mme de Villedieu or Mrs. Manley she did not publish the story of her life romantically disguised as the Secret History of Eliza, nor was there One of the Fair Sex (real or pretended) to chronicle her "strange and surprising adventures" or to print her passion-stirring epistles, as had happened with Mrs. Aphra Behn's fictitious exploits and amorous correspondence.[1] Indeed the first biographer of Mrs. Haywood[2] hints that "from a supposition of some improper liberties being taken with her character after death by the intermixture of truth and falsehood with her history," the apprehensive dame had herself suppressed the facts of her life by laying a "solemn injunction on a person who was well acquainted with all the particulars of it, not to communicate to anyone the least circumstance relating to her." The success of her precaution is evident in the scantiness of our information about her. The few details recorded in the "Biographia Dramatica" can be amplified only by a tissue of probabilities. Consequently Mrs. Haywood's one resemblance to Shakespeare is the obscurity that covers the events of her life.

She was born in London, probably in 1693, and her father, a man by the name of Fowler, was a small shop-keeper.[3] She speaks vaguely of having received an education beyond that afforded to the generality of her sex. Her marriage to Valentine Haywood,[4] a clergyman at least

---

1. E. Bernbaum, *Mrs. Behn's Biography a Fiction*, PMLA, XXVIII, 432.

2. David Erskine Baker, *Companion to the Play House*, 1764.

3. The London Parish Registers contain no mention of an Eliza Fowler in 1693, but on 21 January, 1689, O.S., "Elizabeth dau. of Robert ffowler & Elizabeth his wife" was christened at St. Peter's, Cornhill. Later entries show that Robert was a hosier to his trade. Possibly in suppressing the other particulars of her life, Mrs. Haywood may have consigned to oblivion a year or two of her age, but in her numerous writings I have not found any allusion that could lead to her positive identification with the daughter of Robert Fowler.

4. He was the author of *An Examination of Dr. Clarke's Scripture-Doctrine of the Trinity, with a Confutation of it* (1719). The work is a paragraph by paragraph refutation from the

fifteen years older than his spouse, took place before she was twenty, for the Register of St. Mary Aldermary records on 3 December, 1711, the christening of Charles, son of Valentine Haywood, clerk, and Elizabeth his wife. Her husband held at this time a small living in Norfolk, and had recently been appointed lecturer of St. Mathews, Friday Street. Whether the worthy cleric resided altogether in London and discharged his duties in the country by proxy, or whether Mrs. Haywood, like Tristram Shandy's mother, enjoyed the privilege of coming to town only on certain interesting occasions, are questions which curious research fails to satisfy. At any rate, one of the two children assigned to her by tradition was born, as we have seen, in London.

No other manifestation of their nuptial happiness appeared until 7 January, 1721, on which date the "Post Boy" contained an Advertisement of the elopement of Mrs. Eliz. Haywood, wife of Rev. Valentine Haywood.[5] The causes of Eliza's flight are unknown. Our only knowledge of her temperament in her early life comes from a remark by Nichols that the character of Sappho in the "Tatler"[6] may be "assigned with. . . probability and confidence, to Mrs. Elizabeth Heywood, who. . . was in all respects just such a character as is exhibited here." Sappho is described by Steele as "a fine lady, who writes verses, sings, dances, and can say and do whatever she pleases, without the imputation of anything that can injure her character; for she is so well known to have no passion but self-love, or folly but affectation, that now, upon any occasion, they only cry, 'It is her way!' and 'That is so like her!' without farther reflection." She quotes a "wonderfully just" passage from Milton, calls a licentious speech from Dryden's "State of Innocence" an "odious thing," and says "a thousand good things at random, but so strangely mixed, that you would be apt to say, all her wit is mere good luck, and not the effect of reason and judgment." In the second paper Sappho quotes examples of generous love from Suckling and Milton, but takes

---

authority of scripture of the *Scripture Doctrine of the Trinity* (1712) by the metaphysical Dr. Samuel Clarke, whose unorthodox views prevented Queen Caroline from making him Archbishop of Canterbury. The Reverend Mr. Haywood was upon safe ground in attacking a book already condemned in Convocation.

5. "Whereas Elizabeth Haywood, Wife of the Reverend Mr. Valentine Haywood, eloped from him her Husband on Saturday the 26th of November last past, and went away without his Knowledge and Consent: This is to give Notice to all Persons in general, That if anyone shall trust her either with Money or Goods, or if she shall contract Debts of any kind whatsoever, the said Mr. Haywood will not pay the same."

6. *Tatler*, No. 6 and No. 40.

GEORGE WHICHER

offence at a letter containing some sarcastic remarks on married women. We know that Steele was personally acquainted with Mrs. Manley, and it is possible that he knew Mrs. Haywood, since she later dedicated a novel to him. With some reservation, then, we may accept this sketch as a fair likeness. As a young matron of seventeen or eighteen she was evidently a lively, unconventional, opinionated gadabout fond of the company of similar She-romps, who exchanged verses and specimen letters with the lesser celebrities of the literary world and perpetuated the stilted romantic traditions of the Matchless Orinda and her circle. A woman of her independence of mind, we may imagine, could not readily submit to the authority of an arbitrary, orthodox clergyman husband.

Mrs. Haywood's writings are full of the most lively scenes of marital infelicity due to causes ranging from theological disputes to flagrant licentiousness. Her enemies were not so charitable as to attribute her flight from her husband to any reason so innocent as incompatibility of temper or discrepancy of religious views. The position of ex-wife was neither understood nor tolerated by contemporary society. In the words of a favorite quotation from "Jane Shore":

> "But if weak Woman chance to go astray,
> If strongly charm'd she leave the thorny Way,
> And in the softer Paths of Pleasure stray,
> Ruin ensues, Reproach and endless Shame;
> And one false Step entirely damns her Fame:
> In vain, with Tears, the Loss she may deplore,
> In vain look back to what she was before,
> She sets, like Stars that fall, to rise no more!"

Eliza Haywood, however, after leaving the thorny way of matrimony, failed to carry out the laureate's metaphor. Having less of the fallen star in her than Mr. Rowe imagined, and perhaps more of the hen, she refused to set, but resolutely faced the world, and in spite of all rules of decorum, tried to earn a living for herself and her two children, if indeed as Pope's slander implies, she had children to support.

The ways in which a woman could win her bread outside the pale of matrimony were extremely limited. A stage career, connected with a certain degree of infamy, had been open to the sex since Restoration times, and writing for the theatre had been successfully practiced by

Mrs. Behn, Mrs. Manley, Mrs. Centlivre, Mrs. Pix, and Mrs. Davys. The first two female playwrights mentioned had produced beside their dramatic works a number of pieces of fiction, and Mrs. Mary Hearne, Mrs. Jane Barker, and Mrs. Sarah Butler had already gained a milder notoriety as *romancières*. Poetry, always the elegant amusement of polite persons, had not yet proved profitable enough to sustain a woman of letters. Eliza Haywood was sufficiently catholic in her taste to attempt all these means of gaining reputation and a livelihood, and tried in addition a short-lived experiment as a publisher. Beside these literary pursuits we know not what obscure means for support she may have found from time to time.

Her first thought, however, was apparently of the theatre, where she had already made her debut on the stage of the playhouse in Smock Alley (Orange Street), Dublin during the season of 1715, as Chloe in "Timon of Athens; or, the Man-Hater."[7] One scans the *dramatis personae* of "Timon" in vain for the character of Chloe, until one recalls that the eighteenth century had no liking for Shakespeare undefiled. The version used by the Theatre Royal was, of course, the adaptation by Thomas Shadwell, in which Chloe appears chiefly in Acts II and III as the maid and confidant of the courtesan Melissa. Both parts were added by Og. The rôle of Cleon was taken by Quin, later an interpreter of Mrs. Haywood's own plays. But if she formed a connection with either of the London theatres after leaving her husband, the engagement was soon broken off, and her subsequent appearances as an actress in her comedy of "A Wife to be Lett" (1723) and in Hatchett's "Rival Father" (1730) were due in the one case to an accident and in the other to her friendship for the playwright.

She herself, according to the "Biographia Dramatica," when young "dabbled in dramatic poetry; but with no great success." The first of her plays, a tragedy entitled "The Fair Captive," was acted the traditional three times at Lincoln's Inn Fields, beginning 4 March, 1721.[8] Aaron Hill contributed a friendly epilogue. Quin took the part of Mustapha, the despotic vizier, and Mrs. Seymour played the heroine. On 16 November, it was presented a fourth time for the author's benefit,[9] then allowed to die. Shortly after the first performance the printed

7. W.R. Chetwood, *A General History of the Stage*, 56.
8. Genest, III, 59.
9. Genest, III, 73.

copy made its appearance. In the "Advertisement to the Reader" Mrs. Haywood exposes the circumstances of her turning playwright, naïvely announcing:

"To attempt anything in Vindication of the following Scenes, wou'd cost me more Time than the Composing 'em took me up. . .

"This Tragedy was originally writ by Capt. Hurst, and by him deliver'd to Mr. Rich, to be acted soon after the opening of the New House;[10] but the Season being a little too far elaps'd for the bringing it on then, and the Author oblig'd to leave the Kingdom, Mr. Rich became the Purchaser of it, and the Winter following order'd it into Rehearsal: but found it so unfit for Representation, that for a long time he laid aside all thoughts of making anything of it, till last January, he gave me the History of his Bargain, and made me some Proposals concerning the new modelling it: but however I was prevail'd upon, I cannot say my Inclination had much share in my Consent. . . On Reading, I found I had much more to do than I expected; every Character I was oblig'd to find employment for, introduce one entirely new, without which it had been impossible to have guessed at the Design of the Play; and in fine, change the Diction so wholly, that, excepting in the Parts of Alphonso and Isabella, there remains not twenty lines of the Original."

The plot, which is too involved to be analyzed, centers about the efforts of Alphonso to redeem his beloved Isabella from, the harem of the Vizier Mustapha. Spaniards, Turks, keepers and inhabitants of the harem, and a "young lady disguis'd in the habit of an Eunuch," mingle in inextricable intrigue. Some of the worst absurdities and the most bathetic lines occur in the parts of the two lovers for which Mrs. Haywood disclaims responsibility, but even the best passages of the play add nothing to the credit of the reviser. Her next dramatic venture was produced after her novels had gained some vogue with the town, as the Prologue spoken by Mr. Theophilus Cibber indicates.

---

10. John Rich opened the New Theatre in Lincoln's Inn Fields during December, 1714.

> *"Criticks! be dumb tonight—no Skill display;*
> *A dangerous Woman-Poet wrote the Play: . . .*
> *Measure her Force, by her known Novels, writ*
> *With manly Vigour, and with Woman's wit.*
> *Then tremble, and depend, if ye beset her,*
> *She, who can talk so well, may act yet better."*

The fair success achieved by "A Wife to be Lett: A Comedy," acted at Drury Lane three times, commencing 12 August, 1723,[11] is said to have been due largely to the curiosity of the public to see the author, who by reason of the indisposition of an actress performed in person the part of the wife, Mrs. Graspall, a character well suited to her romping disposition. It is difficult to imagine how the play could have succeeded on its own merits, for the intricacies of the plot tax the attention even of the reader. A certain Ann Minton, however, revived the piece in the guise of "The Comedy of a Wife to be Lett, or, the Miser Cured, compressed into Two Acts" (1802).

Apparently the reception of her comedy was not sufficiently encouraging to induce Mrs. Haywood to continue writing plays, for six years elapsed before she made a third effort in dramatic writing with a tragedy entitled, "Frederick, Duke of Brunswick-Lunenburgh," which was first produced at Lincoln's Inn Fields on 4 March, 1729,[12] and shortly afterward published with a dedication to Frederick Lewis, Prince of Wales. The intention of the dedication was obviously to bid for royal patronage, but the intended victim was too astute to be caught. In eulogizing the Emperor Frederick (*c*. 1400) the author found abundant opportunity to praise by implication his namesake, but unfortunately for the success of the play none of the royal family "vouchsafed to honour it with their Presence." Mrs. Haywood complains that hers "was the only new Performance this Season, which had not received a Sanction from some of that illustrious Line," and the "unthinking Part of the Town" followed the fashion set by royalty. Unlike "The Fair Captive," which suffered from a plethora of incidents, Mrs. Haywood's second tragedy contains almost nothing in its five acts but rant. An analysis of the plot is but a summary of conversations.

---

11. Genest, III, 113.
12. Genest, III, 241.

GEORGE WHICHER

Act I. The German princes hail Frederick, recently elected Emperor. Count Waldec and Ridolpho, in league with the Archbishop of Metz, conspire against him. Waldec urges his sister Adelaid to marry the gallant Wirtemberg. Sophia, her woman and confidant, also urges her to marry, but Adelaid can only reply, "I charge thee Peace, Nor join such distant Sounds as Joy and Wirtemberg," and during the rest of the act proclaims the anguish inspired by her unrequited passion for Frederick, married three years before to a Saxon princess.

Act II. The conspirators plan to kill Frederick. Adelaid reproaches him for abandoning her. He welcomes his imperial consort, Anna, and takes occasion to deliver many magnanimous sentiments.

Act III. Adelaid declares that she cannot love Wirtemberg. Waldec excites the impatient lover to jealousy of Frederick. Ridolpho is banished court for murder.

Act IV. Frederick is distressed by Wirtemberg's discontent. The Empress, seeking to learn the reason for it, is infected by Wirtemberg's suspicions. Adelaid overhears Ridolpho and Waldec plotting to slay Frederick, but hesitates to accuse her own brother. Wirtemberg reproaches her for her supposed yielding to Frederick, and resolves to leave her forever.

Act V. Adelaid, in order to warn him, sends to ask the Emperor to visit her. Waldec intercepts the letter and resolves to murder Frederick in her chamber. Wirtemberg learns that he has been duped and defends the Emperor. Waldec and Ridolpho are killed, though not before they succeed in mortally wounding Frederick, who dies amid tears.

Genest says with truth that the love scenes are dull, and that the subject is not well calculated for dramatic representation. The play was acted only the usual three times, and fully deserved the deep damnation of its taking off.

In 1730 Mrs. Haywood took part in the "Rival Father, or the Death of Achilles," written by her friend, the actor and playwright William Hatchett, and performed at the Haymarket.[13] Three years later she joined with him to produce an adaptation of Fielding's "Tragedy of Tragedies, or the Life and Death of Tom Thumb the Great" on the model of Gay's

---

13. *Biographia Dramatica.* The production is mentioned by Genest, III, 281.

popular "Beggar's Opera." The "Opera of Operas" follows its original closely with a number of condensations and omissions. Almost the only additions made by the collaborators were the short lyrics, which were set to music by the ingenious Mr. Frederick Lampe.[14] The Hatchett-Haywood version was acted at the Haymarket on 31 May, 1733, and according to Genest, was repeated eleven times at least with Mrs. Clive as Queen Dollalolla.[15] It was published immediately. On 9 November, a performance was given at Drury Lane. Although unusually successful, it was Mrs. Haywood's last dramatic offering.[16]

The aspiring authoress apparently never found in dramatic writing a medium suitable to her genius, and even less was she attracted by a stage career. The reasons for her abandoning the theatre to develop her powers as a writer of fiction are stated in a characteristic letter still filed among the State Papers.[17]

Sir

The Stage not answering my Expectation, and the averseness of my Relations to it, has made me Turn my Genius another Way; I have Printed some Little things which have mett a Better Reception then they Deservd, or I Expected: and have now Ventur'd on a Translation to be done by Subscription, the Proposalls whereof I take the Liberty to send You: I have been so much us'd to Receive favours from You that I can make No Doubt of y'r forgiveness for this freedom, great as it is, and that You will alsoe become one of those Persons, whose Names are a Countenance to my undertaking. I am mistress of neither words nor happy Turn

---

14. W.R. Chetwood, *A General History of the Stage*, 57.

15. Genest, III, 408.

16. In Kane O'Hara's later and more popular transformation of Tom Thumb into a light opera, the song put into the mouth of the dying Grizzle by the first adapters was retained with minor changes.

> *"My body's like a bankrupt's shop,*
> *My creditor is cruel death,*
> *Who puts to trade of life a stop,*
> *And will be paid with this last breath; Oh!"*

Apparently O'Hara made no further use of his predecessors.

17. S.P. Dom. George I, Bundle 22, No. 97.

of thought to Thank You as I ought for the many Unmeritted favours You have Conferr'd on me, but beg You to believe all that a gratefull Soul can feel, mine does who am Sir

Yo'r most humble &
most Obedient Serv't
ELIZA HAYWOOD

August ye 5th 1720

Enclosed with the letter were "Proposals For Printing by Subscription A Translation from the French of the Famous Monsieur Bursault Containing Ten Letters from a Lady of Quality to a Chevalier."[18] The work thus heralded was published in the latter part of 1720 by subscription—"three shillings each Book in Quires, or five Shillings bound in Calf, Gilt Back"—a method never again employed by Mrs. Haywood, though in this case it must have succeeded fairly well. Three hundred and nine names appeared on her list of subscribers, of which one hundred and twenty-three were women's. Few subscribers of either sex were distinguished. There were, however, that universal patron of minor authors, George Bubb, Esq., later the Doddington to whom Thomson dedicated his "Summer"; Mrs. Barker, the novelist; Aaron Hill; a Mr. Osborne, possibly the bookseller whose name was afterward infamously connected with Eliza's in "The Dunciad"; Charles de La Faye, the under-secretary of state with whom Defoe corresponded; and a sprinkling of aristocratic titles.

The publisher of the letters was William Rufus Chetwood, later the prompter at Drury Lane Theatre, but then just commencing bookseller at the sign of Cato's Head, Covent Garden. He had already brought out for Mrs. Haywood the first effort of her genius, a romantic tale entitled "Love in Excess: or, the Fatal Enquiry." We have the author's testimony that the three parts "mett a Better Reception then they Deservd," and indeed the piece was extraordinarily successful, running through no less than six separate editions before its inclusion in her collected "Secret Histories, Novels and Poems" in 1725. On the last page of "Letters from a Lady of Quality to a Chevalier" Chetwood had also advertised for

---

18. In spite of the fact that "Translated from the French" appeared on the title-page, Mrs. Haywood has hitherto been accredited with the full authorship of these letters. They were really a loose translation of *Lettres Nouvelles. . . Avec Treize Lettres Amoureuses d'une Dame à un Cavalier* (Second Edition, Paris, 1699) by Edme Boursault, and were so advertised in the public prints.

speedy publication "a Book entitled, The Danger of giving way to Passion, in Five Exemplary Novels: First, The British Recluse, or the Secret History of Cleomira, supposed dead. Second, The Injur'd Husband, or the Mistaken Resentment. Third, Lasselia, or the Unfortunate Mistress. Fourth, The Rash Resolve, or the Untimely Discovery. Fifth, Idalia, or the Self-abandon'd.[19] Written by Mrs. Eliza Haywood." During the next three years the five novels were issued singly by Chetwood with the help of other booksellers, usually Daniel Browne, Jr., and Samuel Chapman. This pair, or James Roberts, Chetwood's successor, published most of Mrs. Haywood's early writings. The staple of her output during the first decade of authorship was the short amatory romance like "Love in Excess" and the "exemplary novels" just mentioned. These exercises in fiction were evidently composed *currente calamo*, with little thought and less revision, for an eager and undiscriminating public. Possibly, as Mr. Gosse conjectures,[20] they were read chiefly by milliners and other women on the verge of literacy. But though persons of solid education avoided reading novels and eastern tales as they might the drinking of drams, it is certain that no one of scanty means could have afforded Mrs. Haywood's slender octavos at the price of one to three shillings. The Lady's Library ("Spectator" No. 37) containing beside numerous romances "A Book of Novels" and "The New Atalantis, with a Key to it," which last Lady Mary Montagu also enjoyed, and the dissolute country-gentleman's daughters ("Spectator" No. 128) who "read Volumes of Love-Letters and Romances to their Mother," a *ci-devant* coquette, give us perhaps a more accurate idea of the woman novelist's public. Doubtless Mrs. Haywood's wares were known to the more frothy minds of the polite world and to the daughters of middle-class trading families, such as the sisters described in Defoe's "Religious Courtship," whose taste for fashionable plays and novels was soon to call the circulating library into being.

Beside the proceeds arising from the sale of her works, Mrs. Haywood evidently expected and sometimes received the present of a guinea or

---

19. Probably a misprint. When the novels appeared, *Idalia* was the Unfortunate Mistress, *Lasselia* the Self-abandon'd. Perhaps because the work outgrew its original proportions, or because short novels found a readier sale, the five were never published under the inclusive cautionary caption.

20. E. Gosse, *Gossip in a Library*, 161, "What Ann Lang Read." Only one of Mrs. Haywood's novels, *The City Jilt*, was ever issued in cheap form. T. Bailey, the printer, evidently combined his printing business with the selling of patent medicines.

so in return for a dedication. Though patrons were not lacking for her numerous works, it does not appear that her use of their names was always authorized. In putting "The Arragonian Queen" under the protection of Lady Frances Lumley, in fact, the author confessed that she had not the happiness of being known to the object of her praise, but wished to be the first to felicitate her publicly upon her nuptials. We may be sure that the offering of "Frederick, Duke of Brunswick-Lunenburgh" to the hero's namesake, Frederick, Prince of Wales, was both unsanctioned and unacknowledged. Sometimes, however, the writer's language implies that she had already experienced the bounty of her patron, while in the case of the novel dedicated to Sir Richard Steele at a time when his health and credit were fast giving way, Eliza can hardly be accused of interested motives. Apparently sincere, too, though addressed to a wealthy widow, was the tribute to Lady Elizabeth Germain prefixed to "The Fruitless Enquiry"; and at least one other of Mrs. Haywood's productions is known to have been in Lady Betty's library. But these instances are decidedly exceptional. Usually the needy novelist's dedications were made up of servile adulation and barefaced begging. With considerable skill in choosing a favorable moment she directed a stream of panegyric upon William Yonge (later Sir) within two months after his appointment as one of the commissioners of the treasury in Great Britain. Soon after Sir Thomas Lombe was made a knight, the wife of that rich silk weaver had the pleasure of seeing her virtues and her new title in print. And most remarkable of all, Lady Elizabeth Henley, who eloped with a rake early in 1728, received Mrs. Haywood's congratulations upon the event in the dedication of "The Agreeable Caledonian," published in June, though if we may trust Mrs. Delany's account of the matter, the bride must already have had time for repentance. Even grief, the specialist in the study of the passions knew, might loosen the purse strings, and accordingly she took the liberty to condole with Col. Stanley upon the loss of his wife while entreating his favor for "The Masqueraders." But of all her dedications those addressed to her own sex were the most melting, and from their frequency were evidently the most fruitful.

The income derived from patronage, however, was at best uncertain and necessitated many applications. To the public, moreover, a novel meant nothing if not something new. Eliza Haywood's productiveness, therefore, was enormous. When she had settled to her work, the authoress could produce little pieces, ranging from sixty to nearly two hundred pages in length, with extraordinary rapidity. In 1724, for instance, a year of tremendous activity, she rushed into print no less than ten original romances, beside translating half of a lengthy French work, "La Belle Assemblée" by Mme de Gomez. At this time, too, her celebrity had become so great that "The Prude, a Novel, written by a Young Lady" was dedicated to her, just as Mrs. Hearne at the beginning of her career had put a romance, "The Lover's Week," under the protection of the famous Mrs. Manley. Between 1720 and 1730 Mrs. Haywood wrote, beside plays and translations, thirty-eight works of her own composing, one in two stout volumes and several in two or more parts. If we may judge by the number and frequency of editions, most of the indefatigable scribbler's tales found a ready sale, while the best of them, such as "Idalia" (1723), "The Fatal Secret" (1724), "The Mercenary Lover" (1726), "The Fruitless Enquiry" and "Philidore and Placentia" (1727), gained for her not a little applause.

Nor was the young adventuress in letters unhailed by literary men. Aaron Hill immediately befriended her by writing an epilogue for her first play and another of Hill's circle, the irresponsible Richard Savage, attempted to "paint the Wonders of Eliza's Praise" in verses prefixed to "Love in Excess" and "The Rash Resolve" (1724).[21]

Along with Savage's first complimentary poem were two other effusions, in one of which an "Atheist to Love's Power" acknowledged his conversion through the force of Eliza's revelation of the tender passion, while the other expressed with less rapture the same idea. But it remained for James Sterling, the friend of Concanen, to state most vigorously the contemporary estimate of Mrs. Haywood and her early writings.[22] "Great Arbitress of Passion!" he exclaims,

> *"Persuasion waits on all your bright Designs,*
> *And where you point the varying Soul inclines:*
> *See! Love and Friendship, the fair Theme inspires*
> *We glow with Zeal, we melt in soft Desires!*
> *Thro' the dire Labyrinth of Ills we share*

---

21. The latter may be read in Savage's Poems, Cooke's edition, II, 162. The complimentary verses first printed before the original issue.

22. His poem *To Mrs. Eliza Haywood on her Writings* was hastily inserted in the fourth volume of *Secret Histories, Novels, and Poems* when that collection had reached its third edition (1732). In the fourth edition of ten years later it stands, with the verses already described, at the beginning of Volume I.

> *The kindred Sorrows of the gen'rous Pair;*
> *Till, pleas'd, rewarded Vertue we behold,*
> *Shine from the Furnace pure as tortur'd Gold:"*

of *Love in Excess*, Part II, and at the front of each successive edition, have never been reprinted. A specimen of his praise follows,

> *"Thy Prose in sweeter Harmony refines,*
> *Than Numbers flowing thro' the Muse's Lines;*
> *What Beauty ne'er could melt, thy Touches fire,*
> *And raise a Musick that can Love inspire;*
> *Soul-thrilling Accents all our Senses wound,*
> *And strike with Softness, whilst they charm with Sound!*
> *When thy Count pleads, what Fair his Suit can fly?*
> *Or when thy Nymph laments, what Eyes are dry?*
> *Ev'n Nature's self in Sympathy appears,*
> *Yields Sigh for Sigh, and melts in equal Tears;*
> *For such Descriptions thus at once can prove*
> *The Force of Language, and the Sweets of Love.*
> *You sit like Heav'n's bright Minister on High,*
> *Command the throbbing Breast, and watry Eye,*
> *And, as our captive Spirits ebb and flow,*
> *Smile at the Tempests you have rais'd below:*
> *The Face of Guilt a Flush of Vertue wears,*
> *And sudden burst the involuntary Tears:*
> *Honour's sworn Foe, the Libertine with Shame,*
> *Descends to curse the sordid lawless Flame;*
> *The tender Maid here learns Man's various Wiles,*
> *Rash Youth, hence dread the Wanton's venal Smiles—*
> *Sure 'twas by brutal Force of envious Man,*
> *First Learning's base Monopoly began;*
> *He knew your Genius, and refus'd his Books,*
> *Nor thought your Wit less fatal than your Looks.*
> *Read, proud Usurper, read with conscious Shame,*
> *Pathetic* Behn, *or* Mauley's *greater Name;*
> *Forget their Sex, and own when* Haywood *writ,*
> *She clos'd the fair Triumvirate of Wit;*
> *Born to delight as to reform the Age,*
> *She paints Example thro' the shining Page;*

Satiric Precept warms the moral Tale,
And Causticks burn where the mild Balsam fails; (sic)
A Task reserv'd for her, to whom 'tis given,
To stand the Proxy of vindictive Heav'n!"

Amid the conventional extravagance of this panegyric exist some useful grains of criticism. One of the most clearly expressed and continually reiterated aims of prose fiction, as of other species of writing from time immemorial, was that of conveying to the reader a moral through the agreeable channel of example. This exemplary purpose, inherited by eighteenth century novelists from Cervantes and from the French romances, was asserted again and again in Mrs. Haywood's prefaces,[23] while the last paragraphs of nearly all her tales were used to convey an admonition or to proclaim the value of the story as a "warning to the youth of both sexes." To modern readers these pieces seem less successful illustrations of fiction made didactic, than of didacticism dissolved and quite forgot in fiction, but Sterling and other eulogists strenuously supported the novelist's claim to moral usefulness.[24] The pill of improvement supposed to be swallowed along with the sweets of diversion hardly ever consisted of good precepts and praiseworthy actions, but usually of a warning or a horrible example of what to avoid.[25] As a

---

23. In the Preface to *Lasselia* (1723), for instance, she feels obliged to defend herself from "that Aspersion which some of my own Sex have been unkind enough to throw upon me, that I seem to endeavour to divert more than to improve the Minds of my Readers. Now, as I take it, the Aim of every Person, who pretends to write (tho' in the most insignificant and ludicrous way) ought to tend at least to a good Moral Use; I shou'd be sorry to have my Intentions judg'd to be the very reverse of what they are in reality. How far I have been able to succeed in my Desires of infusing those Cautions, too necessary to a Number, I will not pretend to determine; but where I have had the Misfortune to fail, must impute it either to the Obstinacy of those I wou'd persuade, or to my own Deficiency in that very Thing which they are pleased to say I too much abound in—a true description of Nature."
24. An eight page verse satire entitled *The Female Dunces. Inscribed to Mr. Pope* (1733) after criticizing the conduct of certain well known ladies, concludes with praise of a nymph who we may believe was intended to represent Eliza Haywood:

"Eliza good Examples shews in vain,
Despis'd, and laugh'd at by the vicious Train;
So bright she shines, she might adorn a Throne
Not with a borrow'd Lustre, but her Own."

25. A single exception was *The Surprise* (1724), dedicated to Steele in the following words: "The little History I presume to offer, being composed of Characters full of Honour and

GEORGE WHICHER

necessary corollary, the more striking and sensational the picture of guilt, the more efficacious it was likely to prove in the cause of virtue. So in the Preface to "Lasselia" (1723), published to "remind the unthinking Part of the World, how dangerous it is to give way to Passion," the writer hopes that her unexceptionable intent "will excuse the too great Warmth, which may perhaps appear in some particular Pages; for without the Expression being invigorated in some measure proportionate to the Subject, 'twou'd be impossible for a Reader to be sensible how far it touches him, or how probable it is that he is falling into those Inadvertencies which the Examples I relate wou'd caution him to avoid." As a woman, too, Mrs. Haywood was excluded from "Learning's base Monopoly," but not from an intuitive knowledge of the passions, in which respect the sex were, and are, thought the superiors of insensible man.[26] Consequently her chief excellence in the opinion of her readers lay in that power to "command the throbbing Breast and watry Eye" previously recognized by the Volunteer Laureate and her other admirers. She could tell a story in clear and lively, if not always correct and elegant English, and she could describe the ecstasies and agonies of passion in a way that seemed natural and convincing to an audience nurtured on French *romans à longue haleine* and heroic plays. Unworthy as they may seem when placed beside the subsequent triumphs of the novel, her short romances nevertheless kept alive the spirit of idealistic fiction and stimulated an interest in the emotions during an age when even poetry had become the handmaid of reason.

But although Eliza had few rivals as an "arbitress of the passions," she did not enjoy an equal success as the "proxy of vindictive heaven." When she attempted to apply the caustic of satire instead of the mild

---

Generosity, I thought I had a fit Opportunity, by presenting it to one who has made it so much his Study to infuse those Principles, and whose every Action is a shining Example of them, to express my Zeal in declaring myself with all imaginable Regard," etc., etc.

26. See the Dedication to *The Fatal Secret* (1724). "But as I am a Woman, and consequently depriv'd of those Advantages of Education which the other Sex enjoy, I cannot so far flatter my Desires, as to imagine it in my Power to soar to any Subject higher than that which Nature is not negligent to teach us. "Love is a Topick which I believe few are ignorant of; there requires no Aids of Learning, no general Conversation, no Application; a shady Grove and purling Stream are all Things that's necessary to give us an Idea of the tender Passion. This is a Theme, therefore, which, while I make choice to write of, frees me from the Imputation of vain or self-sufficient:—None can tax me with having too great an Opinion of my own Genius, when I aim at nothing but what the meanest may perform. "I have nothing to value myself on, but a tolerable Share of Discernment."

balsam of moral tales, she speedily made herself enemies. From the very first indeed she had been persecuted by those who had an inveterate habit of detecting particular persons aimed at in the characters of her fictions,[27] and even without their aspersions her path was sufficiently hard.

> "It would be impossible to recount the numerous Difficulties a Woman has to struggle through in her Approach to Fame: If her Writings are considerable enough to make any Figure in the World, Envy pursues her with unweary'd Diligence; and if, on the contrary, she only writes what is forgot, as soon as read, Contempt is all the Reward, her Wish to please, excites; and the cold Breath of Scorn chills the little Genius she has, and which, perhaps, cherished by Encouragement, might, in Time, grow to a Praise-worthy Height."[28]

Unfortunately the cold breath of scorn, though it may have stunted her genius, could not prevent it from bearing unseasonable fruit. Her contributions to the Duncan Campbell literature, "A Spy upon the Conjurer" (1724) and "The Dumb Projector" (1725), in which the romancer added a breath of intrigue to the atmosphere of mystery surrounding the wizard, opened the way for more notorious appeals to the popular taste for personal scandal. In the once well known "Memoirs of a Certain Island adjacent to the Kingdom of Utopia" (1725–6) and the no less infamous "Secret History of the Present Intrigues of the Court of Carimania" (1727) Mrs. Haywood found a fit repertory for daringly licentious gossip of the sort made fashionable reading by Mrs. Manley's "Atalantis." But though the *romans à clef* of Mrs. Haywood, like the juvenile compositions of Mr. Stepney, might well have "made grey authors blush," her chief claim to celebrity undoubtedly depends upon her inclusion in the immortal ranks of Grubstreet. Her scandal novels did not fail to arouse the wrath of persons in high station, and

---

27. See the Preface to *The Injur'd Husband* quoted in Chap. IV.
28. Preface to *The Memoirs of the Baron de Brosse* (1725). A similar complaint had appeared in the Dedication of *The Fair Captive* (1721). "For my own part. . . I suffer'd all that Apprehension could inflict, and found I wanted many more Arguments than the little Philosophy I am Mistress of could furnish me with, to enable me to stem that Tide of Raillery, which all of my Sex, unless they are very excellent indeed, must expect, when once they exchange the Needle for the Quill."

GEORGE WHICHER

Alexander Pope made of the writer's known, though never acknowledged connection with pieces of the sort a pretext for showing his righteous zeal in the cause of public morality and his resentment of a fancied personal insult. The torrent of filthy abuse poured upon Eliza in "The Dunciad" seems to have seriously damaged her literary reputation. During the next decade she wrote almost nothing, and after her curious allegorical political satire in the form of a romance, the "Adventures of Eovaai" (1736), the authoress dropped entirely out of sight. For six years no new work came from her pen. What she was doing during this time remains a puzzle. She could hardly have been supported by the rewards of her previous labors, for the gains of the most successful novelists at this period were small. If she became a journalist or turned her energies toward other means of making a livelihood, no evidence of the fact has yet been discovered. It is possible that (to use the current euphemism) 'the necessity of her affairs may have obliged her to leave London and even England until creditors became less insistent. There can be little doubt that Mrs. Haywood visited the Continent at least once, but the time of her going is uncertain.[29]

When she renewed her literary activity in 1742 with a translation of "La Paysanne Parvenue" by the Chevalier de Mouhy, Mrs. Haywood did not depend entirely upon her pen for support. A notice at the end of the first volume of "The Virtuous Villager, or Virgin's Victory," as her work was called, advertised "new books sold by Eliza Haywood, Publisher, at the Sign of Fame in Covent Garden." Her list of publications was not extensive, containing, in fact, only two items: I. "The Busy-Body; or Successful Spy; being the entertaining History of Mons. Bigand. . . The whole containing great Variety of Adventures, equally instructive and diverting," and II "Anti-Pamela, or Feign'd Innocence detected, in a Series of Syrena's Adventures: A Narrative which has really its Foundation in Truth and Nature. . . Publish'd as a necessary Caution to all young Gentlemen. The Second Edition."[30] Mrs. Haywood's venture

---

29. See a poem by Aaron Hill, *To Eliza upon her design'd Voyage into Spain* (undated), Hill's *Works*, III, 363. Also *The Husband*, 59. "On a trip I was once taking to France, an accident happen'd to detain me for some days at Dover," etc. Mrs. Haywood's relations with Hill have been excellently discussed by Miss Dorothy Brewster, *Aaron Hill* (1913), 186.
30. The first of these was a translation of the Chevalier de Mouhy's best known work, *La Mouche, ou les Aventures et espiègleries facétieuses de Bigand*, (1730), and may have been done by Mrs. Haywood herself. The second title certainly savors of a typical Haywoodian production, but I have been unable to find a copy of these alleged publications. Neither

as a publisher was transitory, for we hear no more of it. But taken together with a letter from her to Sir Hans Sloane,[31] recommending certain volumes of poems that no gentleman's library ought to be without, the bookselling enterprise shows that the novelist had more strings than one to her bow.

By one expedient or another Mrs. Haywood managed to exist fourteen years longer and during that time wrote the best remembered of her works. Copy from her pen supplied her publisher, Thomas Gardner, with a succession of novels modeled on the French fiction of Marivaux and De Mouhy, with periodical essays reminiscent of Addison, with moral letters, and with conduct books of a nondescript but popular sort. The hard-worked authoress even achieved a new reputation on the success of her "Fortunate Foundlings" (1744), "Female Spectator" (1744–6), and her most ambitious novel, "The History of Miss Betsy Thoughtless" (1751). The productions known to be hers do not certainly represent the entire output of her industry during this period, for since "The Dunciad" her writing had been almost invariably anonymous. One or two equivocal bits of secret history and scandal-mongering may probably be attributed to her at the very time when in "Epistles for the Ladies" (1749–50) she was advocating sobriety, religion, and morality. These suspected lapses into her old habits should serve as seasoning to the statement of the "Biographia Dramatica" that Eliza Haywood was "in mature age, remarkable for the most rigid and scrupulous decorum, delicacy, and prudence, both with respect to her conduct and conversation." If she was not too old a dog to learn new tricks, she at least did not forget her old ones. Of her circumstances during her last years little can be discovered. "The Female Spectator," in emulation of its famous model, commences with a pen-portrait of the writer, which though not intended as an accurate picture, certainly contains no flattering lines. It shows the essayist both conscious of the faults of her youth and willing to make capital out of them.

---

of them was originally published at the Sign of Fame, and they could hardly have been pirated, since Cogan, who issued the volume wherein the advertisement appeared, was also the original publisher of *The Busy-Body*. The *Anti-Pamela* had already been advertised for Huggonson in June, 1741, and had played a small part in the series of pamphlets, novels, plays, and poems excited by Richardson's fashionable history. If Mrs. Haywood wrote it, she was biting the hand that fed her, for *The Virtuous Villager* probably owed its second translation and what little sale it may have enjoyed to the similarity between the victorious virgin and the popular Pamela.

31. B.M. (Mss. Sloane. 4059. ff. 144), undated.

GEORGE WHICHER

"As a Proof of my Sincerity, I shall, in the first place, assure him (the reader), that for my own Part I never was a Beauty, and am now very far from being young; (a Confession he will find few of my Sex ready to make): I shall also acknowledge that I have run through as many Scenes of Vanity and Folly as the greatest Coquet of them all.—Dress, Equipage, and Flattery were the Idols of my Heart.—I should have thought that Day lost, which did not present me with some new Opportunity of shewing myself.—My Life, for some Years, was a continued Round of what I then called Pleasure, and my whole Time engross'd by a Hurry of promiscuous Diversions.—But whatever Inconveniences such a manner of Conduct has brought upon myself, I have this Consolation, to think that the Publick may reap some Benefit from it:—The Company I kept was not, indeed, always so well chosen as it ought to have been, for the sake of my own Interest or Reputation; but then it was general, and by Consequence furnished me, not only with the Knowledge of many Occurrences, which otherwise I had been ignorant of, but also enabled me. . . to see into the most secret Springs which gave rise to the Actions I had either heard, or been Witness of—to judge of the various Passions of the Human Mind, and distinguish those imperceptible Degrees by which they become Masters of the Heart, and attain the Dominion over Reason. . .

"With this Experience, added to a Genius tolerably extensive, and an Education more liberal than is ordinarily allowed to Persons of my Sex, I flatter'd myself that it might be in my Power to be in some measure both useful and entertaining to the Publick."

A less favorable glimpse of the authoress and her activities is afforded by a notice of a questionable publication called "A Letter from H——G—— g, Esq." (1750), and dealing with the movements of the Young Chevalier. It was promptly laid to her door by the "Monthly Review."[32]

"The noted Mrs. H—— d, author of four volumes of novels well known, and other romantic performances, is the reputed author of this pretended letter; which was privately conveyed to the

32. *Monthly Review*, II, 167, Jan. 1750.

shops, no publisher caring to appear in it: but the government, less scrupulous, took care to make the piece taken notice of, by arresting the female veteran we have named; who has been some weeks in custody of a messenger, who also took up several pamphlet-sellers, and about 800 copies of the book; which last will now probably be rescued from a fate they might otherwise have undergone, that of being turned into waste-paper, . . . by the famous fiery nostrum formerly practised by the physicians of the soul in *Smithfield*, and elsewhere; and now as successfully used in *treasonable*, as then in *heretical* cases."

This unceremonious handling of the "female veteran," in marked contrast to the courteous, though not always favorable treatment of Mrs. Haywood's legitimate novels, suggests the possibility that even the reviewers were ignorant of the authorship of "The History of Jemmy and Jenny Jessamy" (1753) and "The Invisible Spy" (1755). Twenty years later, in fact, a writer in the "Critical Review" used the masculine pronoun to refer to the author of "Betsy Thoughtless." It is quite certain that Mrs. Haywood spent the closing years of her life in great obscurity, for no notice of her death appeared in anyone of the usual magazines. She continued to publish until the end, and with two novels ready for the press, died on 25 February, 1756.[33]

"In literature," writes M. Paul Morillot, "even if quality is wanting, quantity has some significance," and though we may share Scott's abhorrence for the whole "Jemmy and Jenny Jessamy tribe" of novels, we cannot deny the authoress the distinction accorded her by the "Biographia Dramatica" of being—for her time, at least—"the most voluminous female writer this kingdom ever produced." Moreover, it is not Richardson, the meticulous inventor of the epistolary novel, but the past-mistress of sensational romance who is credited with originating the English domestic novel. Compared with the delicate perceptions and gentle humor of Fanny Burney and Jane Austen, Mrs. Haywood's best volumes are doubtless dreary enough, but even if they only crudely foreshadow the work of incomparably greater genius, they represent an advance by no means slight. From "Love in Excess" to "Betsy

33. The *Biographia Dramatica* gives this date. Clara Reeve, *Progress of Romance*, I, 121, however, gives 1758, while Mrs. Griffith, *Collection of Novels* (1777), II, 159, prefers 1759. The two novels were *Clementina* (1768), a revision of *The Agreeable Caledonian*, and *The History of Leonora Meadowson* (1788).

Thoughtless" was a step far more difficult than from the latter novel to "Evelina." As pioneers, then, the author of "Betsy Thoughtless" and her obscurer contemporaries did much to prepare the way for the notable women novelists who succeeded them. No modern reader is likely to turn to the "Ouida" of a bygone day—as Mr. Gosse calls her—for amusement or for admonition, but the student of the period may find that Eliza Haywood's seventy or more books throw an interesting sidelight upon public taste and the state of prose fiction at a time when the half created novel was still "pawing to get free his hinder parts."

II

Short Romances of Passion

The little amatory tales which formed Mrs. Haywood's chief stock in trade when she first set up for a writer of fiction, inherited many of the characteristics of the long-winded French romances. Though some were told with as much directness as any of the intercalated narratives in "Clélie" or "Cléopâtre," others permitted the inclusion of numerous "little histories" only loosely connected with the main plot. Letters burning with love or jealousy were inserted upon the slightest provocation, and indeed remained an important component of Eliza Haywood's writing, whether the ostensible form was romance, essay, or novel. Scraps of poetry, too, were sometimes used to ornament her earliest effusions, but the other miscellaneous features of the romances—lists of maxims, oratory, moral discourses, and conversations—were discarded from the first. The language of these short romances, while generally more easy and often more colloquial than the absurd extravagances of the translators of heroic romances and their imitators, still smacked too frequently of shady groves and purling streams to be natural. Many conventional themes of love or jealousy, together with such stock types as the amorous Oriental potentate, the lover disguised as a slave, the female page, the heroine of excessive delicacy, the languishing beauty, the ravishing sea-captain, and the convenient pirate persisted in the pages of Mrs. Barker, Mrs. Haywood, and Mrs. Aubin. As in the interminable tomes of Scudéry, love and honor supplied the place of life and manners in the tales of her female successors, and though in some respects their stories were nearer the standard of real conduct, new novel on the whole was but old romance writ small.

In attempting to revitalize the materials and methods of the romances Mrs. Haywood was but following the lead of the French *romancières*, who had successfully invaded the field of prose fiction when the passing of the précieuse fashion and Boileau's influential ridicule[1] had discredited the romance in the eyes of writers with

---

1. *Les Héros de Roman*, 1664, circulated in Ms. and printed in 1688 without the consent of the author. Not included in Boileau's *Works* until 1713.

GEORGE WHICHER

classical predilections. Mme de La Fayette far outshines her rivals, but a host of obscure women, headed by Hortense Desjardins, better known as Mme de Villedieu, hastened to supply the popular demand for romantic stories. In drawing their subjects from the histories of more modern courts than those of Rome, Greece, or Egypt they endeavored to make their "historical" romances of passion more lifelike than the heroic romances, and while they avoided the extravagances, they also shunned the voluminousness of the *romans à longue haleine*. So the stories related in "La Belle Assemblée" by Mme de Gomez, translated by Mrs. Haywood in 1725 and often reprinted, are nearer the model of Boccaccio's novelle than of the Scudéry romance, both in their directness and in being set in a framework, but the inclusion, in the framework, of long conversations on love, morals, politics, or wit, with copious examples from ancient and modern history, of elegant verses on despair and similar topics, and of such miscellaneous matter as the "General Instructions of a Mother to a Daughter for her Conduct in Life," showed that the influence of the salon was not yet exhausted. In the continuation called "L'Entretien des Beaux Esprits" (translated in 1734), however, the elaborate framework was so far reduced that fourteen short tales were crowded into two volumes as compared with eighteen in the four volumes of the previous work. Writers of fiction were evidently finding brief, unadorned narrative most acceptable to the popular taste.

That the "novels" inserted in these productions had not ceased to breathe the atmosphere of romance is sufficiently indicated by such titles as "Nature outdone by Love," "The Triumph of Virtue," "The Generous Corsair," "Love Victorious over Death," and "Heroick Love." French models of this kind supplied Mrs. Haywood with a mine of romantic plots and situations which she was not slow to utilize.[2] Furthermore, her natural interest in emotional fiction was quickened by these and other translations from the French. The "Letters from a Lady of Quality to a Chevalier" emphasized the teaching of the "Lettres Portugaises," while "The Lady's Philosopher's Stone; or, The

---

2. The story of Tellisinda, who to avoid the reproach of barrenness imposes an adopted child upon her husband, but later bearing a son, is obliged to see a spurious heir inherit her own child's estate, was borrowed with slight changes from La Belle Assemblée, I, Day 5, and used in Mrs. Haywood's *Fruitless Enquiry*, (1727).

Caprices of Love and Destiny" (1725),[3] although claiming to be an "historical novel" in virtue of being set "in the time, when Cromwell's Faction prevail'd in England," was almost entirely occupied with the matters indicated in the sub-title. And in "The Disguis'd Prince: or, the Beautiful Parisian" (1728) she translated the melting history of a prince who weds a merchant's daughter in spite of complicated difficulties.[4] Much reading in books of this sort filled Mrs. Haywood's mind with images of exalted virtue and tremendous vice, and like a Female Quixote, she saw and reported the life about her in terms borrowed from the romances. So, too, Mrs. Manley had written her autobiography in the character of Rivella.

This romantic turn of mind was not easily laid aside, but the women writers made some progress toward a more direct and natural representation of the passions. The advance was due partly, no doubt, to a perception of the heroic absurdities of French fiction, but also to the study of Italian *novelle* and the "Exemplary Novels" of Cervantes. But even when imitating the compression of these short tales Mrs. Haywood did not always succeed in freeing herself from the "amour trop delicat" of the romantic conventions. In two short "novels" appended to "Cleomelia: or, the Generous Mistress" (1727) the robust animalism of the Italian tales comes in sharp contrast with the *délicatesse* of the French tradition. "The Lucky Rape: or, Fate the best Disposer" illustrates the spirit of the *novelle*.

Emilia, rusticated to Andalusia to escape falling in love, gives her heart to Berinthus, whom she meets at a masquerade. On her way to a second entertainment to meet her lover, her terror of a drunken cavalier induces her to accept the protection of the amorous Alonzo and paves the way for her ruin. Berinthus turns out to be her brother Henriquez. Alonzo, his friend, marries the lady as soon as her identity is discovered, and all parties are perfectly content.

Though the scene of "The Capricious Lover: or, No Trifling with a Woman" is likewise laid in Spain, the atmosphere of the story is far different.

---

3. *La Pierre philosophale des dames, ou les Caprices de l'amour et du destin*, by Louis Adrien Duperron de Castera, (1723), 12mo.

4. *L'Illustre Parisienne*, (1679), variously attributed to Préchac and to Mme de Villedieu, had already been translated as *The Illustrious Parisian Maid, or The Secret Amours of a German Prince*, (1680). A synopsis is given by H.E. Chatenet, *Le Roman et les Romans d'une femme de lettres. . . Mme de Villedieu*, (Paris, 1911), 253–9.

Montano, doubtful of Calista's affection for him, feigns to break with her, and she, though really loving him, returns an indifferent answer and marries Gaspero out of pique. The distracted lover thereupon falls upon his sword in the presence of the newly wedded couple, and the bride, touched by the spectacle of her lover's devotion, languishes and dies in a few months.

There is little naturalness in the extravagant passion of the second story, but until sensationalism cloyed the public palate, realism was an unnecessary labor. By placing the events in some romantic country like Spain, Portugal, Italy, or even France, any narrative of excessive love could be made to pass current. The Latin countries were vaguely imagined by romantic novelists as a sort of remote but actual *pays du Tendre* where the most extraordinary actions might occur if only "love, soft love" were the motivating force.

A collection of select novels called "Love in its Variety," advertised in 1727 as "Written in Spanish by Signior Michel Ban Dello; made English by Mrs. Eliza Haywood," was apparently a translation from the *novelle* of Matteo Bandello, probably from a French version.[5] The best examples of her brief, direct tales, however, are to be found in "The Fruitless Enquiry. Being a Collection of several Entertaining Histories and Occurrences, which Fell under the Observation of a Lady in her Search after Happiness" (1727). Although the scene is laid in Venice, the model of this framework story was probably not the "Decameron" but the Oriental tales, known in England through French translations and imitations of the "Arabian Nights." Intercalated stories were not uncommon in French romances, but they were almost invariably introduced as life histories of the various characters. A fantastic framework, with a hint of magic, fabricated expressly to give unity to a series of tales, half exemplary, half satirical, points directly to an ultimate connection with the narratives of Scheherezade and Sutlememé. No attempt to catch the spirit of the East is discernible, but the vogue of Oriental tales was evidently beginning to make an impression on French and English writers of fiction. Care for the moral welfare of her readers doubtless influenced Mrs. Haywood to assert in the dedication to Lady Elizabeth Germain that the following "Sheets... contain the History of some real Facts," and that the author's chief design in publishing was to "persuade my Sex from seeking Happiness the wrong Way."

---

5. I have not seen a copy of the book.

At any rate the moral of the stories suited the taste of the age.[6]

Miramillia, widow of a nobleman in Venice, loses her only son, and is informed by a soothsayer that she will hear nothing of him until she has a shirt made for him by a woman perfectly content. She, therefore, seeks among her acquaintance for the happy woman, but one after another reveals to her a secret disquiet.

Anziana, married against her will to the Count Caprera, encourages her former lover, Lorenzo, to continue his friendship for her. Her husband and father, believing that she is about to prove faithless to her marriage vows, secretly assassinate Lorenzo, and cause his skeleton to be set up in Anziana's closet for an object lesson. When she discovers it, she refuses to be reconciled to her husband, and vows to spend an hour a day weeping over Lorenzo's remains.

On the night of his marriage Montrano is torn from the arms of Iseria by his cruel uncle and shipped to Ceylon. Shipwrecked, he becomes the slave of a savage Incas, whose renegade Italian queen falls in love with him. But neither her blandishments nor the terrible effects of her displeasure can make him inconstant to Iseria. After suffering incredible hardships, he returns to see Iseria once more before entering a monastery, but she, loyal even to the semblance of the man, refuses to allow him to leave her.

Stenoclea's doting parents refuse to let her wed Armuthi, a gentleman beneath her in fortune, and he in hopes of removing the objection goes on his travels. Her parents die, her brother is assassinated on his way home to Venice, she becomes mistress of her fortune, and soon marries her lover. Completely happy, she begins to make a shirt for Miramillia's son, but before it is completed, a servant who had been wounded when her brother was killed, returns and identifies Armuthi as the slayer. Through Miramillia's influence the husband is pardoned, but Stenoclea retires to a convent.

An adventuress named Maria boasts to Miramillia that she has attained perfect felicity by entrapping the Marquis de Savilado into

---

6. Mrs. E. Griffith's comment on the work is typical of the tendency to moralize even the amusements of the day. See *A Collection of Novels*, (1777), II, 162. "The idea on which this piece is founded, has a good deal of merit in it; as tending to abate envy, and conciliate content; by shewing, in a variety of instances, that appearances are frequently fallacious; that perfect or permanent happiness is not the lot of mortal life; and that peace of mind and rational enjoyment are only to be found in bosoms free from guilt, and from intimate connection with the guilty."

a marriage. She too undertakes the shirt, but in a few days Miramillia hears that the supposed Marquis has been exposed as an impostor and turned into the street with his wife.

Violathia endures for a long time the cruelties of her jealous husband, Count Berosi, but finally yields to the persistent kindness of her lover, Charmillo. Just as he has succeeded in alienating his wife's affections, Berosi experiences a change of heart. His conduct makes the divorce impossible, and she is forced to remain the wife of a man she loathes, and to dismiss Charmillo who has really gained her love.

Tellisinda, to avoid the reproach of barrenness, imposes an adopted boy on her husband, but shortly afterward gives birth to a child. She is forced to watch a spurious but amiable heir inherit the estate of her own ill-natured son. (Cf. footnote 2 at end of this chapter.)

Even unmarried ladies, Miramillia finds, are not without their discontents. Amalia is vexed over the failure of a ball gown. Clorilla is outranked by an acquaintance whose father has obtained preferment. Claribella pouts because a man has shot himself for love of her rival. Selinda mourns her lap-dog dead.

Just as Miramillia is ready to give over her search for a happy woman, Adario, her son, returns in company with a former lover of hers whose daughter he has saved from a villain at the expense of a wound from which he has but then recovered. Naturally the girl rewards him with her hand, and all ends well.[7]

Of the stories in this diversified collection that of Anziana approaches in kind, though not in degree, the tragic pathos of Isabella and the Pot of Basil ("Decameron," IV, 5). The second narrative has all the glamor of adventure in the barbaric East, and the romantic interest that attaches to lovers separated but eternally constant. The histories of Stenoclea and of Tellisinda contain situations of dramatic intensity. But perhaps the story of Violathia is the most worthy of attention on account both of its defects and of its merits. The weakest part of the plot is the husband, who is jealous without cause, and equally without reason suddenly reforms. But the character of Violathia is admirably drawn. Unlike the usual heroine of Haywoodian fiction she is superior to circumstance and does not yield her love to the most complacent adjacent male. As a dutiful wife she resists for a long time the insinuations of Charmillo, but when she decides to fly to her lover, her husband's tardy change of

---

7. I have omitted two or three unessential stories in the analysis.

heart cannot alter her feelings. Her character is individual, firm, and palpable. If the story was original with Mrs. Haywood, it shows that her powers of characterization were not slight when she wished to exert them. The influence of the *novella* and of the Oriental tale produced nothing better.

From other literary forms the makers of fiction freely derived sensational materials and technical hints. Without insisting too closely upon the connection between novel and play, we may well remember that nearly all the early novelists, Defoe excepted, were intimately associated with the theatre. Mrs. Behn, Mrs. Manley, Mrs. Haywood, and later Fielding and Mrs. Lennox were successful in both fields. The women writers especially were familiar with dramatic technique both as actors and playwrights, and turned their stage training to account when they wrote prose fiction. Mrs. Haywood's first novel, "Love in Excess" (1720), showed evidences of her apprenticeship to the theatre. Its three parts may be compared to the three acts of a play; the principal climax falls properly at the end of the second part, and the whole ends in stereotyped theatrical fashion with the marriage of all the surviving couples. The handling of incident, too, is in the fashion of the stage. Mrs. Haywood had sufficient skill to build up a dramatic situation, but she invariably solves it, or rather fails to solve it, by an interruption at the critical moment, so that the reader's interest is continually titillated. Of a situation having in itself the germs of a solution, she apparently had not the remotest conception. When a love scene has been carried far enough, the coming of a servant, the sound of a duel near by, or a seasonable outbreak of fire interrupts it. Such devices were the common stock in trade of minor writers for the theatre. Dramatic hacks who turned to prose fiction found it only a more commodious vehicle for incidents and scenes already familiar to them on the stage. In their hands the novel became simply a looser and more extended series of sensational adventures. Accident, though tempered in various degrees by jealousy, hatred, envy, or love, was the supreme motivating force.

The characters of Mrs. Haywood's "Love in Excess" also inherited many traits from the debased but glittering Sir Fopling Flutters, Mirabells, Millamants, and Lady Wishforts of the Restoration stage. Of character drawing, indeed, there is practically none in the entire piece; the personages are distinguished only by the degree of their willingness to yield to the tender passion. The story in all its intricacies may best be described as the *vie amoureuse* of Count D'Elmont, a hero with none of the wit, but with all the gallantry of the rakes of late Restoration comedy. Two parts of the novel relate the aristocratic intrigues of D'Elmont and his friends; the third shows him, like Mrs. Centlivre's gallants in the fifth act, reformed and a model of constancy. It would be useless to detail the sensational extravagances of the plot in all its ramifications, but the hero's adventures before and after marriage may serve as a fair sample of the whole.

D'Elmont, returning to Paris from the French wars, becomes the admiration of both sexes, but especially in the eyes of the rich and noble Alovisa appears a conquest worthy of her powers. To an incoherent expression of her passion sent to him in an anonymous letter he pays no attention, having for diversion commenced an intrigue with the lovely Amena. Though Alovisa in a second billet bids him aim at a higher mark, "he had said too many fine things to be lost," and continues his pursuit until Amena's father takes alarm and locks her up. Through her maid she arranges for a secret meeting, and though touched by her father's reproofs, she is unable to withstand the pleas of the captivating count. Their tete-a-tete in the Tuilleries, however, is interrupted by Alovisa's spies, who alarm the house with cries of fire, so that the lovers find themselves locked out. Half senseless with dismay, Amena finds shelter in the house of Alovisa, who, though inwardly triumphant, receives her rival civilly and promises to reconcile her to her father. D'Elmont is so patently glad to be relieved of his fair charge that she demands back her letter, but he by mistake gives her one of Alovisa's, whose handwriting she immediately recognizes. When the polite Count returns to enquire after her health, she accuses her lover and friend of duplicity, faints, and letting fall Alovisa's letter from her bosom, brings about an *éclaircissement* between D'Elmont and that lady. Before Amena's recovery the Count hastens away to welcome his brother, and when the imprudent girl has been safely lodged in a convent, D'Elmont, moved more by ambition than by love, weds the languishing Alovisa.

After his marriage the Count soon quarrels with his wife and consoles himself by falling in love with his ward, the matchless Melliora, but the progress of his amour is interrupted by numerous unforeseen accidents. The mere suspicion of his inconstancy raises his wife's jealousy to a fever heat. To expose her rival she pretends to yield to the persuasions of her wooer, the Baron D'Espernay, but as a result of a very intricate intrigue both Alovisa and the Baron perish accidentally on the swords of D'Elmont and his brother.

Melliora retires to a convent, and her lover goes to travel in Italy, where his charms cause one lady to take poison for love of him, and another to follow him disguised as the little foot-page Fidelio. In helping Melliora's brother to elope with a beautiful Italian girl, the Count again encounters his beloved Melliora, now pursued by the Marquis de Sanguillier. In a dramatic *dénouement* she deserts the Marquis at the altar and throws herself upon the protection of her guardian. The disappointed bridegroom is consoled by the discovery of an old flame who has long been serving him secretly in the capacity of chambermaid. Fidelio reveals her identity and dies of hopeless love, pitied by all. The three surviving couples marry at once, and this time the husbands "continue, with their fair Wives, great and lovely Examples of conjugal Affection."

Such, with the omission of all secondary narratives, is the main plot of Eliza Haywood's first novel.

"Love in Excess" best illustrates the similarity of sensational fiction to clap-trap drama, but others of her early works bear traces of the author's familiarity with the theatre. The escape of the pair of lovers from an Oriental court, already the theme of countless plays including Mrs. Haywood's own "Pair Captive," was re-vamped to supply an episode in "Idalia" (1723), and parts of the same novel are written in concealed blank verse that echoes the heroic Orientalism of some of Dryden's tragedies. In the character of Grubguard, the amorous alderman of "The City Jilt" (1726), Mrs. Haywood apparently had in mind not Alderman Barber, whom the character little resembles, but rather Antonio in Otway's "Venice Preserved." And the plot of "The Distressed Orphan, or Love in a Mad-House" (c. 1726), where young Colonel Marathon feigns himself mad in order to get access to his beloved Annilia, may perhaps owe its inspiration to the coarser mad-house scenes of Middleton's "Changeling." [8] On the whole, however, the drama but poorly repaid its debt to prose fiction.

An indication of the multifarious origins of the short tales of love is to be found in the nominal diversity of the setting. The scene, though often laid in some such passion-ridden land as Spain or Italy, rarely affects the nature of the story. But as in such novels as "Philidore and

8. Act I, sc. ii. In the novel the heroine is shut up by a miserly hunks of an uncle to force her into a detested mercenary match with his son. In the play the mistress is the wife of the old and jealous keeper of the asylum.

GEORGE WHICHER

Placentia" and "The Agreeable Caledonian" the characters wander widely over the face of Europe and even come in contact with strange Eastern climes, so the writers of romantic tales ransacked the remotest corners of literature and history for sensational matter. The much elaborated chronicle of the Moors was made to eke out substance for "The Arragonian Queen" (1724), a story of "Europe in the Eighth Century," while "Cleomelia: or, the Generous Mistress" was advertised as the "Secret History of a Lady Lately Arriv'd from Bengall." The tendency to exploit the romantic features of outlandish localities was carried to the ultimate degree by Mrs. Penelope Aubin, whose characters range over Africa, Turkey, Persia, the East and West Indies, and the North American continent, often with peculiar geographical results. But neither Mrs. Aubin nor Mrs. Haywood was able to use the gorgeous local color that distinguished Mrs. Behn's "Oroonoko," and still less did they command the realistic imagination that could make the travels of a Captain Singleton lifelike.

Even when, as in "The Mercenary Lover," the setting is transferred to "the Metropolis of one of the finest Islands in the World," and the action takes place "in the neighborhood of a celebrated Church, in the Sound of whose Bells the Inhabitants of that populous City think it an Honour to be born,"[9] the change is unaccompanied by any attempt at circumstantial realism. We are told that Belinda of "The British Recluse" is a young lady of Warwickshire, that Fantomina follows her lover to Bath in the guise of a chambermaid, or that "The Fair Hebrew" relates the "true, but secret history of two Jewish ladies who lately resided in London," but without the labels the settings could not be distinguished from the vague and unidentified *mise en scène* of such a romance as "The Unequal Conflict." Placentia in England raves of her passion for Philidore exactly as Alovisa in Paris, Emanuella in Madrid,[10] or Cleomelia in Bengal expose the raptures and agonies of their passions. The hero of "The Double Marriage" (1726) rescues a distressed damsel in the woods outside of Plymouth exactly as one of Ariosto's or Spenser's knights-errant might have done in the fairy country of old romance. In the sordid tale of "Irish Artifice," printed in Curll's "Female Dunciad" (1728), no reader could distinguish in the romantic names Aglaura and Merovius the nationality or the meanness

---

9. Preface to *The Mercenary Lover*, (1726).
10. *The Rash Resolve*, (1724).

of a villainous Irish housekeeper and her son. And though the tale is the very reverse of romantic, it contains no hint of actual circumstance. The characters in Mrs. Haywood's early fiction move in an imaginary world, sometimes, it is true, marked with the names of real places, but no more truly realistic than the setting of "Arcadia" or "Parthenissa."

Nor are the figures that people the eighteenth century paradise of romance more definitely pictured than the landscape. They are generally unindividualized, lay figures swayed by the passions of the moment, or at best mere "humour" characters representing love's epitome, extravagant jealousy, or eternal constancy. Pope could make a portrait specific by the vigorous use of epigrams, but Mrs. Haywood's comments on her heroes and heroines are but feeble. The description of Lasselia, for instance, contains no trait that is particular, no characteristic definitely individual. The girl is simply the type of all that is conventionally charming in her sex, "splendidly null, dead perfection."

> "But if the grave Part of the World were charm'd with her Wit and Discretion, the Young and Gay were infinitely more so with her Beauty; which tho' it was not of that dazzling kind which strikes the Eye at first looking on it with Desire and Wonder, yet it was such as seldom fail'd of captivating Hearts most averse to Love. Her features were perfectly regular, her Eyes had an uncommon Vivacity in them, mix'd with a Sweetness, which spoke the Temper of her Soul; her Mien was gracefully easy, and her Shape the most exquisite that could be; in fine, her Charms encreas'd by being often seen, every View discover'd something new to be admir'd; and tho' they were of that sort which more properly may be said to persuade than to command Adoration, yet they persuaded it in such a manner, that no Mortal was able to resist their Force." (p. 2.)

Mrs. Haywood's heroes are merely the masculine counterparts of her women. Bellcour, the type of many more, "had as much Learning as was necessary to a Gentleman who depended not on that alone to raise his Fortune: He had also admirable Skill in Fencing, and became a Horse as well as any Man in the World."[11] Victor over a thousand hearts, the Haywoodian male ranges through his glittering sphere, ever

---

11. *The Double Marriage*, (1726).

ready to fall in or out of love as the occasion demands. D'Elmont of "Love in Excess" possesses a soul large enough to contain both love and fury at almost the same moment. A "brulée" with his spouse merely increases his tenderness for his ward.

"You have done well, Madam, (said D'Elmont, looking on her with Eyes sparkling with Indignation) you have done well, by your impertinent Curiosity and Imprudence, to rouze me from my Dream of Happiness, and remind me that I am that wretched thing a Husband! 'Tis well indeed, answer'd Alovisa, (who saw now that there was no need of farther Dissimulation) that anything can make you remember, both what you are, and what I am. You, resum'd he, hastily interrupting her, have taken an effectual Method to prove your self a Wife!—a very Wife!—Insolent—Jealous—and Censorious!—But Madam, continued he frowning, since you are pleased to assert your Privilege, be assur'd, I too shall take my turn, and will exert the—Husband! In saying this, he flung out of the Room in spite of her Endeavours to hinder him, and going hastily through a Gallery which had a large Window that look'd into the Garden, he perceiv'd Melliora lying on a green Bank, in a melancholy but a charming Posture, directly opposite to the place where he was; her Beauties appear'd, if possible more to advantage than ever he had seen them, or at least he had more opportunity thus unseen by her, to gaze upon them: he in a moment lost all the Rage of Temper he had been in, and his whole Soul was taken up with Softness. . . Ambition, Envy, Hate, Fear, or Anger, every other Passion that finds entrance in the Soul, Art and Discretion may disguise; but Love, tho' it may be feign'd, can never be conceal'd, not only the Eyes (those true and most perfect Intelligencers of the Heart) but every Feature, every Faculty betrays it! It fills the whole Air of the Person possess'd of it; it wanders round the Mouth! plays in the Voice! trembles in the Accent! and shows itself a thousand different ways! even Melliora's care to hide it, made it more apparent; and the transported D'Elmont, not considering where he was, or who might be a witness of his Rapture, could not forbear catching her in his Arms, and grasping her with an extasy, which plainly told her what his thoughts were, tho' at that time he had not power to put 'em into words; and indeed there is no greater Proof of a vast and elegant Passion, than the being uncapable of expressing it." (p. 79.)

Oddly enough the early experimenters in fiction never perceived that to seem real a passion must be felt by a real person. They attempted again and again to heighten the picture of envy, fear, ambition, rage, or love by all manner of extraordinary circumstances, but they rarely succeeded in attaching the emotion to a lifelike character. It was indeed passion, but passion painted on the void, impalpable. Consequently they almost never succeeded in maintaining complete verisimilitude, nor was their character drawing any less shadowy than in the sentimental romances of Sidney and Lodge. Compare, for example, the first expression of Rosalynde's love with the internal debate of Mrs. Haywood's Placentia.[12] Both are cast in soliloquy form, and except that the eighteenth century romancer makes no attempt to decorate the style with fantastic conceits, the two descriptions are not essentially different.

"(Placentia) was no sooner at liberty to reflect, than she grew amazed at herself for having expresd, and still feeling so uncommon a Concern for the Service she had received from Jacobin (Philidore); he did no more, said she, than was his Duty, nay, any Man would have done as much for a Woman to whom he had not the least obligation, if distressed and assaulted in the manner she had been—why then, continued she, does the action appear so charming, so meritorious from him?—'Tis certainly the surprize to find so much gallantry and courage in a Man of his mean birth, that has caused this disorder in my Soul—were he my Equal I should think it was Love had seized me, but Oh! far be it from me to debase myself so far—Yet, again would she retort, what can I wish in Man that is not to be found in this too lovely Slave? . . . Besides, who knows but that his Descent may be otherwise than he pretends—I have heard of Princes who have wandered in strange disguises—he may be in reality as far above me as he seems beneath. . . The thought that there was a possibility for such a thing to be, had no sooner entered into her head than she indulged it with an infinity of rapture, she painted him in Imagination the most desperate dying Lover that ever was, represented the transports she shou'd be in when the blest discovery shou'd be made, held long discourses with him, and formed answers such as she supposed he wou'd make on such an occasion. Thus, for

---

12. Lodge's *Rosalynde, ed.* E.C. Baldwin, p. 19. *Philidore and Placentia* (1727), p. 12.

some hours did she beguile her Cares, but Love, who takes delight sometimes to torment his Votarys wou'd not long permit her to enjoy this satisfaction... Reason, with stern remonstrances checked the Romantick turn of her late thoughts, and showed her the improbability of the hope she had entertained: Were he, cryed she, with an agony proportioned to her former transports, of any degree which you'd encourage his pretensions to my Love, he cou'd not for so long a Time have endured the servile Offices to which he has been put—Some way his ingenious passion wou'd have found out to have revealed itself—No, no, he is neither a Lover nor a Gentleman, and I but raise Chimera's to distract myself... but Ill (*sic*) retrieve all yet, Ill discharge him from my house and service—he is an Enchanter, and has bewitched me from my Reason, and never, never more shall he behold my face."

The normal character in Eliza Haywood's tales almost invariably conformed to some conventional type borrowed from the romance or the stage. The author's purpose was not to paint a living portrait, but to create a vehicle for the expression of vivid emotion, and in her design she was undoubtedly successful until the reading public was educated to demand better things.

On exception, however, to the customary conventionality of Mrs. Haywood's heroines ought to be noted. Ordinarily the novelist accepted the usual conception of man the pursuer and woman the victim, but sometimes instead of letting lovely woman reap the consequences of her folly after the fashion of Goldsmith's celebrated lyric, she violated romantic tradition by making her disappointed heroines retire into self-sufficient solitude, defying society. In real life the author of these stories was even more uncompromising. Far from pining in obscurity after her elopement from her husband, she continued to exist in the broad light of day, gaining an independent living by the almost unheard of occupation (as far as women were concerned) of writing. If she was blighted, she gave no indication of the fact. Something of the same defiant spirit actuated the unfortunate Belinda and Cleomira of "The British Recluse" (1722).

Belinda, a young lady of fortune in Warwickshire, comes to London on business and meets at her lodging-house a mysterious fair recluse. Imagining that their lots may be somewhat akin, she induces the retired beauty to relate the history of her misfortunes.

Cleomira upon her father's death is removed from the court to the country by a prudent mother. She does not take kindly to housewifery, and languishes until friends persuade her mother to let her attend a ball. There she meets the glorious Lysander, and in spite of her mother's care, runs away to join him in London. Her ruin and desertion inevitably follow. The sight of a rival in her place makes her frantically resolve to die by poison, but the apothecary gives her only a harmless opiate. Thinking herself dying, she sends a last letter to her faithless lover. When she awakes and hears how indifferently he has received the report of her death, she at length overcomes her unhappy passion, and retires from the world.

Belinda then relates how her marriage with the deserving Worthly was postponed by her father's death. In the interim the captivating Sir Thomas Courtal has occasion to render her a slight service at the overturn of her coach, and fires her with a passion which her mild esteem for Worthly is too weak to overcome. Courtal perceives and encourages her fondness, though he poses as Worthly's friend. She gives him an assignation in a wood, where she is saved from becoming a victim to his lust only by the timely arrival of her true admirer. In the duel that ensues Worthly falls, Courtal flees, and a little later Belinda goes to London in hopes of seeing him. At the playhouse she is only too successful in beholding him in a box accompanied by his wife and mistress. From the gossip of her friends she learns that his real name is Lord——, and from one of the ladies she hears such stories of his villainy that she can no longer doubt him to be a monster.

Worthly, meanwhile, has recovered from his wound and weds Belinda's sister. Lysander and Courtal prove to be in reality the same bland villain, the inconstant Bellamy. His two victims, sympathizing in their common misfortune, agree to retire together to a remote spot where they can avoid all intercourse with the race of men. "And where a solitary Life is the effect of Choice, it certainly yields more solid Comfort, than all the publick Diversions which those who are the greatest Pursuers of them can find."

The same admirable sentiment was shared by the surviving heroine of "The Double Marriage: or, the Fatal Release" (1726), who after witnessing a signal demonstration of the perfidy of man, resolves to shun forever the false sex.

Dazzled by the numerous accomplishments of Bellcour, the charming Alathia weds him in secret. When he finds that his father has designed to bestow his hand upon the heiress of an India merchant, he dares not confess his fault, but lets himself be carried to Plymouth to meet his intended bride. There he determines to escape from his father during a hunting party, but while passing a wood, he hears cries and rescues a fair maiden from violation. The beautiful stranger allows him to conduct her back to Plymouth, and turns out to be Mirtamene, the woman he is to marry. Though very much in love with this new beauty, Bellcour cannot relinquish the thought of Alathia without a struggle. But in fatal hesitation the time slips by, and he is finally compelled to wed a second bride. Meanwhile the deserted Alathia hears disquieting reports of her husband's conduct. In disguise as a boy she travels to Plymouth to see for herself, confronts her guilty partner, and after hearing his confession, stabs herself. Overcome by remorse and love, Bellcour imitates her, while Mirtamene "warn'd by the example of Bellcour, that Interest, Absence, or a new Passion, can make the most seeming constant Lover false, took a Resolution ever to contemn and hate that betraying Sex to which she owed her Misfortune and the Sight of such a Disaster as she had beheld in Alathia."

Not content to retire in disgust from the world, Glicera, the victim of fickle man in "The City Jilt" (1726) determines to retaliate upon the lover who has ruined and abandoned her when the death of her father left her without a fortune or a protector. To secure her revenge she encourages the advances of a senile alderman, Grubguard by name, whom she takes infinite delight in deceiving by the help of an ingenious confidant. Meanwhile an unfortunate lawsuit and the extravagances of his wife have ruined the false Melladore, who is obliged to mortgage his estate to Grubguard. Glicera obtains the deeds from the amorous alderman, and then sends him packing. Melladore is forced to beg of her sufficient funds to purchase a commission and later dies in battle. With the fortune she has won from her various lovers Glicera retires from the world and henceforth shuns the society of men.

In these three tales Mrs. Haywood followed the guidance of her own experience when it ran counter to the traditions of romance. The betrayed heroine ought to have died, or at least to have been immured in a convent to suffer a living death, but instead of acquiescing in their fate, Belinda and Cleomira, Mirtamene, and Glicera defy the world, and in the last case prove that the worm may turn.

Among the works of her first decade of authorship a few effusions in which Mrs. Haywood has succeeded to a degree in motivating, characterizing, or analyzing the passions of her characters, must be exempted from the general charge of commonplaceness. The first of these is "Idalia: or, the Unfortunate Mistress" (1724), the story of a young Venetian beauty—like Lasselia, her charms can only be imagined not described—whose varied amorous adventures carry her over most of Italy.

She is sought by countless suitors, among them the base Florez, whom her father promptly forbids the house. Idalia's vanity is piqued at the loss of a single adorer, and more from perverseness than from love she continues to correspond with him. He makes no further use of her condescension than to boast of her favors, until at the command of his patron, Don Ferdinand, he induces Idalia to make an assignation with him. Ferdinand meets her and not without difficulty at length effects her ruin. Her lover's friend, Henriquez, in conducting her to a place of safety in Padua, becomes himself the victim of her charms, quarrels with Ferdinand, and slays him and is slain. Henriquez' brother, Myrtano, next succeeds as Idalia's adorer, but learning that he is about to make an advantageous marriage, she secretly decamps. In her flight the very guide turns out to be a noble lover in disguise. When she escapes from him in a ship bound for Naples, the sea-captain pays her crude court, but just in time to save her from his embraces the ship is captured by Barbary corsairs—commanded by a young married couple. Though the heroine is in peasant dress, she is treated with distinction by her captors. Her history moves them to tears, and they in turn are in the midst of relating to her the involved story of their courtship, when the vessel is wrecked by a gale. Borne ashore on a plank, Idalia is succored by cottagers, and continues her journey in man's clothes. She is loved by a lady, and by the lady's husband, who turns out to be her dear Myrtano. Their felicity is interrupted by the jealousy of Myrtano's wife, who appeals to the Pope and forces the lovers to separate by his order. Idalia leads a miserable life, persecuted by all the young gallants of Rome. One day she sees Florez, the first cause of all her misfortunes, pass the window, and with thoughts bent on revenge sends him a billet, which he carries to his master. Myrtano keeps the appointment, muffled in a cloak, and Idalia stabs him by mistake. Overcome by remorse, she dies by the same knife.

The motivation of the heroine at the beginning of the story, as Miss Morgan has pointed out,[13] is more elaborate than usual in Haywoodian

---

13. Miss C.E. Morgan, *The Novel of Manners*, (1911), 100.

GEORGE WHICHER

romance. To show a young girl's vanity teasing her into an intrigue required a more delicate appreciation of the passions than the stock situations in love stories afforded. Obliged to draw upon her own resources, Mrs. Haywood handled the incidents with a niceness that could hardly have been expected from the author of "Love in Excess." Her sense for *vraisemblance* protected her from many absurdities, though not from all. For instance, when Idalia to preserve herself from the importunities of Ferdinand employs the same threat of stabbing herself that Clarissa Harlowe in similar circumstances holds over Lovelace, the Italian heroine very naturally tries first to stab her seducer. But realism vanishes when Idalia begins her romantic flight from place to place and from lover to lover. The incidents of romance crowd fast around her. When in man's clothes she is loved by a woman who takes her for what she seems, and by the woman's husband who knows her for what she is, the reader cannot help recalling a similar Gordian love-knot in Sidney's "Arcadia." Perhaps the only convincing detail in the latter part of the book is the heroine's miserable end. But although the sentiments of the characters are reported in concealed blank verse that smacks of theatrical rant, though the absurd Oriental digressions, the disguises, the frequent poisonings, and fortunate accidents all detract from the naturalness and plausibility of the tale, yet one cannot deny the piece occasional merits, which if smothered in extravagances, are hopeful signs of a coming change. The very excess of strained and unnatural incidents indicates that the popular palate was becoming cloyed; for a time the writers of fiction attempted to stimulate it by spicing the dish, but when the limit of mordancy was reached, a new diet became imperative.

Though in no sense a soothing draught for the overstrained sensibilities of romance readers, "The Fatal Secret: or, Constancy in Distress" (1724) nevertheless represents a valuable part of Mrs. Haywood's contribution to the technique of the novel. Few of her works indicate more clearly her power to display the operations of passion dominating a young and innocent heart.

When the story opens, Anadea is a heart-free maid of sixteen, better educated than most young girls, and chiefly interested in her studies. Fearing to leave her unprovided for, her father urges her to marry, and she, though inclined to a single life, returns a dutiful answer, begging him to direct her choice. He fixes upon the worthy Chevalier de Semar, and bids her prepare for the wedding.

"The Time which the necessary Preparations took up, Anadea pass'd in modelling her Soul, as much as possible, to be pleas'd with the State for which she was intended.—The Chevalier had many good Qualities, and she endeavoured to add to them in Imagination a thousand more. Never did any Woman take greater Pains to resist the Dictates of Desire, than she did to create them. . . yet she had it not in her Power to feel any of those soft Emotions, those Impatiencies for his Absence, those tender Thrillings in his Presence, nor any of those agreeable Perplexities which are the unfailing Consequences of Love. . . and she began, at length, to lay the Blame on her own want of Sensibility, and to imagine she had not a Heart fram'd like those of other Women."

At the house of a friend Anadea meets the Count de Blessure and feels the starts of hitherto unsuspected passion. Beside this new lover the Chevalier appears as nought. Her mind is racked by an alternation of hope and despair.

"In Anxieties, such as hopeless Lovers feel, did the discontented Anadea pass the Night:—She could not avoid wishing, though there was not the least Room for her to imagine a Possibility of what she wish'd:—She could not help praying, yet thought those Prayers a Sin.—Her once calm and peaceful Bosom was now all Hurry and Confusion:—The Esteem which she had been long labouring to feel for the Chevalier, was now turn'd to Aversion and Disdain; and the Indifference she had for all Mankind, now converted into the most violent Passion for one. . . she thought she could be contended to live a single Life, and knew so little of the encroaching Nature of the Passion she had entertained, that she believed she should never languish for any greater Joy, than that she might, without a Crime, indulge Contemplation with the Idea of his Perfections; and to destroy that pleasing Theory by marrying with another. . . was more terrible to her than the worst of Deaths.—Confounded what to do, or rather wild that there was nothing she could do that might be of Service to her in an Exigence like this, her Mind grew all a Chaos, and the unintermitting Inquietudes of her Soul not permitting any Repose, she. . . had a very good Pretence to keep her Chamber, and receive no Visits."

She passes the day in tormenting perplexities, sometimes relieved by intervals of unsubstantial joy, when she fancies that her affianced may break off the match for some reason, that his sickness, an accident, or death may leave her free to wed Blessure. In imagination she pictures to herself happy meetings with her lover, and even repeats their conversation. Then recollecting her true situation, she lapses into real woe and bitterness of heart. The Count, however, has been deeply affected by her charms, and though he learns that she is engaged to De Semar, he sends her an appealing letter to discover whether the match is the result of choice or duty. Upon the receipt of this billet the soul of Anadea is distracted between the impulses of love and the dictates of prudence. Finally she writes a discreet, but not too severe reply, intimating that her choice is due more to duty than to inclination. Naturally the Count protests vehemently against her sacrificing herself to a man for whom she cares nothing, vows that the day of her wedding with De Semar shall be his last upon earth, and entreats a meeting.

"What now became of the enamour'd Anadea? How was it possible for a Heart so prepossessed as hers, to hold out in a Reserve which was very near breaking the Strings which held it— . . . Yet still the Consequences that might attend this Meeting, for a Time repelled the Dictates of her Passion.—But it was no more than a faint Struggle; Love! all-conquering, all-o'er-powering Love! triumphed over every other Consideration! and she consented to his and her own impatient Wishes."

Under the pretence of a change of air she goes to a friend's house at Versailles, where Blessure secretly weds her. After a short period of felicity, they are betrayed by an officious maid. Blessure kills the Chevalier, but is himself wounded and cast into prison. His father secures a pardon by promising the king's mistress that the Count shall marry her daughter, but Blessure remains constant to Anadea, though keeping his marriage a secret for fear of infuriating his father. He is sent away by his displeased parent to learn the virtue of obedience, while Anadea retires to St. Cloud to await her husband's return. There the story ends in an unexpected tragedy of incest and blood.

The back-stairs intrigues and the sensational horrors which to the majority of Mrs. Haywood's readers doubtless seemed the chief attraction of the story are not different from the melodramatic features of countless other amatory tales, French and English. But when for a dozen pages the author seeks to discover and explain the motives of her characters both by impersonal comment and by the self-revelation of letters, she is making a noteworthy step—even if an unconscious one—toward the Richardsonian method of laying bare the inner natures of ordinary people. She has here pursued the analysis of character as an end in itself, for in "The Fatal Secret" there is no hint of disguised scandal, nor any appeal to the pruriency of degenerate readers. Sensational in the extreme the story is, but nevertheless the progress of the narrative is delayed while the sentiments of the heroine are examined in the minutest detail. While better known romancers exploited chiefly the strange and surprising adventures (other than amorous) of their characters, or used the *voyage imaginaire* for the purposes of satire, Eliza Haywood and her female colleagues stimulated the popular taste for romances of the heart. In trying to depict the working of intense human passions they rendered a distinct service to the development of English fiction.

The story of "The Mercenary Lover" (1726) involved, besides the ability to body forth emotion, considerable power to show a gradual degradation in the character of one of the heroines.

The avaricious Clitander gains the moiety of a fortune by marrying the young, gay Miranda, but cannot rest without securing to himself the portion of the elder sister as well. Althea's thoughtful and less volatile nature has hitherto resisted the assaults of love, but her insidious brother-in-law undermines her virtue by giving her wanton books and tempting her with soft speeches until she yields to his wishes. When he attempts to make her sign a deed of gift instead of a will to provide for their child, she discovers his treachery and flees to the country. By playing upon her tenderness he coaxes her back and poisons her. Miranda is fully informed of her husband's villainy, but contents herself with removing from the house. Thus Clitander loses not only his sister-in-law's, but his wife's fortune as well, and is completely unmanned by remorse and apprehension.

The contrast between the characters of the gay and thoughtless wife and the pensive, pure-minded girl is skilfully managed, and the various steps in the downward course of Althea's nature are exhibited in detail. Like Anadea in "The Fatal Secret" she retires to her chamber not to sleep, but to indulge in the freedom of her thoughts, which are poured forth at length to let the reader into the secrets of her passion-ridden bosom. To reveal character in action was beyond the limit of Eliza Haywood's

GEORGE WHICHER

technique; and once the story is well under way, Althea becomes as colorless as only a heroine of romance can be. But the author's effort to differentiate the female characters before the action begins, and to make a portion of the plot turn upon a psychological change in one of them shows that even sensation-loving readers were demanding a stricter veracity of treatment than had hitherto been necessary.

But perhaps the most careful interlocking of character and event to be found among these embryo novels is contained in "The Life of Madam De Villesache. Written by a Lady, who was an Eye-witness of the greatest part of her Adventures, and faithfully Translated from her French Manuscript. By Mrs. Eliza Haywood" (1727). Since no original source for this story has come to light, we may probably assume that the French manuscript was a complete fabrication on the part of the English author. At any rate, the tale was one of passion and intrigue such as she delighted to compose.

Henrietta, daughter of a certain Duke, grows up in obscure circumstances to be a miracle of beauty. When her father comes to carry her to court, her rustic lover, Clermont, pleads so effectually that she consents to a secret union with him. In the glare of the court she half forgets her country husband until too fatally reminded of him by being sought in marriage by the Marquis of Ab——lle. Her attempts at evasion are vain, and rather than face her father's anger, she permits herself to be married a second time. She has not long enjoyed her new rank when Clermont, whom she has informed of her step, appears to reproach her and to claim his rights. Still irresolute, she persuades him by tears and prayers not to expose her perfidy, and secretly admits him to a husband's privileges. In due time the pair are caught by the Marquis, and to avoid his rage confess their prior marriage. Clermont is thrown into prison, where he dies not without suspicion of poison. Henrietta retires to convent, but the Duke, her father, in order to gain the Marquis's estate for her unborn infant, manages to stifle the evidence of her first marriage. Enraged that he cannot obtain a divorce, the Marquis resolves to be revenged upon his perjured wife. He intercepts her coach in a wood outside of Paris and brutally murders her. The Duke orders her magnificently buried. Although nothing against the Marquis can be proved, he is not allowed to escape the vengeance of heaven, but goes mad and in a lucid interval just before death confesses his crimes.

The weakness and irresolution of the heroine are made the pivot of each turning point in the plot. When she yields to her lover's entreaties to consummate a hasty marriage; when fear of her father's displeasure induces her to keep their union a secret; when her love of luxurious grandeur at court persuades her to contract a more exalted match; when her terror of Clermont forces her into a shameless expedient for the sake of mollifying his anger; and when after her exposure by her husband, the Marquis, she brazens out her trial in hopes of maintaining the splendor of her rank and fortune, she is welding link by link the chain of circumstance that draws her to ultimate disaster. She is by no means a simple heroine motivated by the elementary passions; instead she is constantly swayed by emotions and desires of the most diverse and complex nature. After her first taste of court life she learns to look back on her husband's rusticity with a sort of contempt, and to regret her precipitate action.

> "Not that she hated Clermont; on the contrary, she had yet very great Remains of her former Passion for him, whenever she reflected on the Endearments which had past between them: but then she depis'd the Meanness of his Extraction, and the Thoughts that she had put him in possession of a Title, which gave him the Power, whenever he pleas'd to exert it, of calling her from the present Grandeur of her State, and obliging her to live with him in a mean Retirement; made all Desires instigated by her Affection, immediately give way to that new Idol of her Wishes, Greatness! And she more ardently endeavour'd to find some Stratagem to prevent him from ever seeing her again, than she had formerly pray'd in the Simplicity and Innocence of her Affections, never to be separated from him." (p. 14).

When an ambitious marriage is proposed, her first horror at the thought of deserting her country husband yields to a sort of resignation when she persuades herself of the necessity of the step. And when she considers the riches, title, and agreeable person of the Marquis, she almost disdains herself for hesitating to prefer him to Clermont. Her life is the tragedy of a soul too indolent to swim against the current of events. Mrs. Haywood managed to give extraordinary vividness and consistency to the character of the vacillating Henrietta by making the plot depend almost entirely upon the indecision of the heroine. Consequently none of the author's women are as sharply defined as this weak, pleasure-loving French girl. The character drawing, though too much subordinated to the sensational elements in the story, is nevertheless distinct and true to life.

Most probably, however, the few attempts at analysis of character or interrelation of character and plot were of little concern both to the author of emotional fiction and to her readers. The romancer's purpose was not to reveal an accurate picture of life and manners, but to thrill the susceptible bosom by scenes of tender love, amorous rapture, or desperate revenge. The department of sensationalism especially exploited by women writers and generally allowed to be most suited to their genius is sufficiently indicated by the words typographically emphasized on the title-page of one of Mrs. Haywood's few essays. "Reflections on the Various Effects of LOVE, According to the contrary Dispositions of the Persons on whom it operates. Illustrated with a great many Examples of the good and bad Consequences of that PASSION. Collected from the best Ancient and Modern HISTORIES. Intermix'd with the latest AMOURS and INTRIGUES of Persons of the First Rank of both Sexes, of a certain Island adjacent to the Kingdom of Utopia. Written by the Author of The Mercenary Lover, and the Memoirs of the said Island. Love is not sin, but where 'tis sinful Love. Never before made Publick." To any contemporary connoisseur of hectic literature such a feast of Love, Passion, Histories, Amours, and Intrigues as this, offered in the shop of N. Dobb in the Strand for the small price of one shilling, must have been irresistible. No less moving was the appeal of Eliza's fiction to such Biddy Tipkins and Polly Honeycombes as delighted in a tale of amorous adventure, particularly if it was set in the glittering atmosphere of the court. A typical story of intrigues among the great is "Lasselia: or, the Self-Abandoned" (1723).

The heroine, niece of Madame de Montespan, finding herself in danger of becoming her aunt's rival in the affections of Louis XIV, goes secretly into the country to visit her friends M. and Mme Valier, where she falls in love with De L'Amye, a married gentleman. Summoned back to court by the amorous monarch, Lasselia chooses rather to flee from the protection of her friends in the disguise of a pilgrim, and led by lucky chance casts herself on the protection of her lover, who conveys her to a country inn and there maintains her for sometime to their mutual felicity. Mile Douxmourie, once affianced to De L'Amye but jilted by him, accidentally discovers the pair and immediately communicates with the gallant's wife, who with the Valiers soon appears to reclaim the recreants. The wife rages at her husband, he at the perfidious Douxmourie, while Lasselia offers to stab herself. By the good offices of her friends, however, the girl is persuaded to enter a nunnery where she becomes a pattern of piety. De L'Amye is reconciled to his wife.

In the first few pages of the story the author makes a noteworthy attempt to create an atmosphere of impending disaster. When De L'Amye first meets the heroine, three drops of blood fall from his nose and stain the white handkerchief in her hand, and the company rallies him on this sign of an approaching union, much to his wife's discomfiture. The accident and her yet unrecognized love fill Lasselia's mind with uneasy forebodings. "She wou'd start like one in a Frenzy, and cry out, Oh! it was not for nothing that those ominous Drops of Blood fell from him on my Handkerchief!—It was not for nothing I was seiz'd with such an unusual Horror—Nor is it in vain, that my Soul shrinks, and seems to dread a second Interview!—They are all, I fear, too sure Predictions of some fatal Consequence." These gloomy thoughts at length give way to an ecstasy of despairing love, and when her affection is reciprocated, to a series of passionate letters and poems, which indeed make necessary the author's apology for the "too great Warmth" of the style.

Since the ultimate disaster of adventurous heroines was regarded as a sop to moral readers, Mrs. Haywood frequently failed to gratify her audience with a happy ending, but occasionally a departure from strict virtue might be condoned, provided it took place in a country far removed from England. The scene of "The Padlock: or, No Guard without Virtue"[14] was appropriately laid in Spain.

Don Lepidio of Seville, by his jealous conduct, completely alienates the affections of his young and beautiful wife, Violante. She finally writes a reply to the earnest entreaties of an unknown lover, and though filled with apprehension at seeing her letter carried off by an ugly black slave, agrees to meet him. Don Honorius, for it was he who had assumed the disguise of the slave, proves to be the wonder of his sex. He persuades her to elope to the house of one of his relations, and after Lepidio has secured a divorce, marries her with great felicity.

That novels of intrigue, even without the tinsel of court dress and the romance of French or Spanish setting, were acceptable to Eliza Haywood's public is shown by the two parts of "The Masqueraders: or,

---

14. A companion-piece to the third edition of *The Mercenary Lover*, (1728).

GEORGE WHICHER

Fatal Curiosity" (1724–5), which in the most luscious language of passion narrate the philanderings of a "charming Rover" called Dorimenus, "whose real Name, for some Reasons, I shall conceal." London masquerades, as the title indicates, play a large part in the plot. A more sprightly tale, though still of the unedifying sort, is "Fantomina: or, Love in a Maze. Being the Secret History of an Amour between two Persons of Condition." The story is so fantastic that it can hardly be suspected of having any connection with an actual occurrence, but the novelist was not unaware of the advertising value of hinted scandal.

A young lady of distinguished birth, beauty, wit, and spirit for a frolic goes masked to the theatre, and there falling in love with the agreeable Beauplaisir, begins an intrigue with him. When his ardor cools, she lures him on again under a different disguise, and thus manages four several *liaisons* successively as Fantomina, Celia the Chambermaid, the Widow Bloomer, and the fair Incognita. Meanwhile she meets her lover frequently in public assemblies without ever arousing his suspicion of her double, or rather manifold identity. But at length she is unable to disguise the effects of her imprudence, her gallant ungallantly refuses to marry her, and the fair intriguer is packed off to a convent in France.

Though the story cannot pretend to support the cause of morality, the style of this piece is unusually clear and straightforward, sometimes suitably periphrastic, but never inflated. The passion described is that of real life ungarnished by romance. Only greater refinement was needed to make the entertainment fit for ladies and gentlemen.

The cardinal defect of some of Mrs. Haywood's romances-in-little lay, however, in a romantic over-refinement of the passions rather than in a too vigorous animalism. Full of the most delicate scruples is "The Surprise: or, Constancy Rewarded" (1724),[15] appropriately dedicated to the Sir Galahad of comedy, Sir Richard Steele. The story relates how Euphemia discovers that the seemingly faithless Bellamant has, in reality, abandoned her on the day set for their marriage because he was unwilling to have her share in the loss of his fortune. She, meanwhile, has inherited a convenient sum, redeems him from his creditors, and after practicing a little mystification to test his constancy, leads him to the altar. Few of Mrs. Haywood's novels are more entirely moral or more essentially dull.

---

15. A companion-piece to *The Fatal Secret: or, Constancy in Distress*.

Though the scene of "The Rash Resolve: or, the Untimely Discovery" (1724) is laid in Porto Rico and in Spain, the romancer took little advantage of her opportunity to introduce the usual "cloak and sword" incidents of Spanish fiction. Instead her tale is one of generous love and melting pathos more characteristic of the romance than of the *novella* or its successors.

The Porto Rican heiress, Emanuella, is defrauded of her fortune by her guardian, Don Pedro, and imprisoned in his house to force her to marry his son, Don Marco. That generous lover helps her to escape to Madrid, and to emphasize the truth of her claims against his wily father, falls upon his sword in the presence of the court. Emanuella's title to her fortune cleared by this extraordinary measure, she continues to reside at the house of Don Jabin, whose daughter, Berillia, she saves from a monastery by making up the deficiency in her dowry. The ungrateful girl, however, resents Emanuella's disapproval of her foppish lover, and resolves to be revenged upon her benefactress. She, therefore, forwards Emanuella's affair with Emilius until the lovers are hopelessly compromised; then taking advantage of the loss of the lady's fortune at sea, blackens her character to Emilius and provokes him to desert her. The abandoned Emanuella enters a convent.

Emilius is challenged by Octavio as a rival in the love of Julia, and though he had never before heard of the lady, he soon becomes her lover in fact, and eventually marries her. Emanuella escapes from the nunnery and wanders to a little provincial town where she bears a son to Emilius. Berillia, who has been rusticated to a village near by in consequence of her amour, encounters her unfortunate friend by chance and runs away from her duenna to join her. She persuades Emanuella to draw a large sum on Don Jabin, robs her, and goes to join her gallant. The injured lady supports her child by mean drudgery until by chance she meets Emilius and his wife, who do all they can to comfort her. But worn out by her afflictions, she dies of a broken heart, leaving her son to be adopted by his father.

Dr. Johnson might with equal truth have said to Mrs. Haywood as to the author of the "Memoirs of Miss Sydney Biddulph," "I know not, Madam, that you have a right. . . to make your readers suffer so much." Even the pathetic "History of Jemmy and Jenny Jessamy" has nothing to surpass the train of woes exhibited in this earlier tale.

In the same "soft" style are two novels, "The Unequal Conflict: or, Nature Triumphant" (1725) and its sequel, "Fatal Fondness: or, Love its own Opposer." The plot begins with the writer's favorite situation.

Philenia, affianced to Coeurdemont, falls in love with Fillamour. By the help of a confidant, Antonia, the lovers are enabled to arrange a plan of escape. On the eve of the wedding Fillamour breaks into the house and, leaving his servants to bind and gag the father, flies immediately to his soul's adored.

"He threw himself on his knees, as he approach'd the dear mistress of his soul, and with a voice and manner all soft and love-inspiring.— Now madam, said he, if the adoring Fillamour is not unworthy the glory of your deliverance, I come to offer it, and to assure you, that not only this, but the service of my whole future life is entirely devoted to you. The innocent Philenia had not presently the power of replying, the different emotions of love, and shame, fear, and joy, made such a confusion in her sentiments, that she could only look the meanings of them all: Fillamour, however, found enough in this mute language to make him know, he was in as fair a way of happiness, as he cou'd wish; and returning her glances with others as languishing, as the most melting longing love cou'd teach the loveliest eyes in the world, they continued, for some moments, thus transmitting souls—" until their confidant hurries them out of the house.

After the elopement Fillamour is distracted by the opposing motives of love and interest. To marry Philenia means ruin, for his ambitious uncle, who has proposed an advantageous marriage to him, would never forgive him for a love match. The innocent cause of his distress finally discovers his perplexity and agrees to live a single life until they can marry without loss of fortune. In this state of affairs "their love seem'd to be a copy of that pure and immaterial passion, which angels regard each other with, and, which we are allow'd to hope shall be our portion, when, shaking off our earth, we meet in a happier world, where we are to live and love forever." The lovers' paradise is invaded by Philenia's father, who carries her home and locks her up more closely than before. In a short time she has the shocking intelligence that Fillamour has married according to the wishes of his worldly uncle. She still remains constant to him, but "the remainder of her yet surprising adventures," remarks the author, "and those of Antonia and Coeurdemont must be told another time, having good reason to doubt my reader will be tir'd, when I am so myself."

Eliza was perhaps the first to recover from the fatigue, for in a little more than two months the continuation, costing sixpence more than the first instalment, was offered to her readers.

After making his marriage of *convenance* Fillamour again pays his court to Philenia, and seizing a lucky moment to surprise her on her daily walk, half by persuasion, half by force, carries his point. But before they can meet a second time she is carried off by a gang of villains, who mistake her for another woman. The languishing Misimene, who has pursued Fillamour into the country in man's clothes, consoles him for the loss of his first love. Upon his return to town he finds that his wife has fled to join her lover. Meanwhile Philenia's honor is preserved by timely shipwreck of the vessel in which the ravishers are carrying her off. Washed ashore on the inevitable plank, she supports herself among the fisher folk by weaving nets until after a year's toil she is relieved by Antonia and Coeurdemont, now happily married. The relation of their adventures occupies some pages. Philenia comes back to town to find her lover weltering in his blood, stabbed by the jealous Misimene. Believing him dead, she seizes the same sword, plunges it into her bosom, and instantly expires. Misimene goes into frenzies, and Fillamour alone recovers to live out a life of undying grief.

"Thus was the crime of giving way to an unwarrantable passion, punish'd in the persons of Philenia and Misimene, and that of perjury and ingratitude in Fillamour; while the constancy of Antonia, and the honour of Coeurdemont, receiv'd the reward their virtues merited, and they continued, to their lives end, great and shining examples of conjugal affection."

Apparently Philenia's adventures were somewhat too improbable even for the taste of readers steeped in melodramatic romances, for if we may judge by the few copies that have survived, these effusions did not enjoy a wide popularity. But not to be discouraged by failure, Mrs. Haywood soon produced another extravagant and complicated romance, entitled "Cleomelia: or, the Generous Mistress. Being the Secret History of a Lady Lately arriv'd from Bengall" (1727). The scene might equally well have been laid in the Isle of Wight, but Bengal on the title-page doubtless served to whet the curiosity of readers.

Gasper, secretly affianced to Cleomelia, is conveyed out of Bengal by an avaricious father to prevent him from marrying, and she, believing him unfaithful, gives her hand to the generous Heartlove. Informed of the truth by a letter from her lover announcing his speedy return, she boards a ship bound for England, leaving her husband and lover to fight

GEORGE WHICHER

a duel in which Heartlove falls. Meanwhile the heroine is shipwrecked, finds a new suitor in the ship's captain, and hearing of her husband's death and of Gasper's marriage to a Spanish lady, marries the captain. Hardly has he departed on his first voyage, when the still faithful Gasper returns to claim her, only to find her again the bride of another. In despair he goes to England, and when her second husband is lost at sea, she follows to reward his constancy.

Cleomelia's generosity does not seem to be as notable as the subtitle would indicate, but the story was evidently intended to illustrate virtues exalted to a high romantic level.

With the same end in view Mrs. Haywood attempted an even loftier flight into the empyrean of romance, with the result that "Philidore and Placentia: or, L'Amour trop Delicat" (1727) is more conventional and stilted than any other work from her pen. It imitates closely the heroic French romances, both in the inflated style and elaborate regard for the tender passion, and in the structure of the plot with little histories of the principal characters interspersed at intervals throughout the story. In substance the tale is simply a mosaic of romantic adventures, though some of the hero's wanderings in the desert after being marooned by pirates and especially his encounter with the "tyger" sound like a faint echo of "Captain Singleton" or of Captain John Smith's "True Travels."

The noble Philidore falls in love with the rich and beautiful Placentia, but as his estate is no match for hers, he contents himself with entering her service in disguise and performing menial offices for the pleasure of seeing her. One day she hears him singing in a grotto, and is charmed by the graceful replies he makes to her questions. A little later he saves her from robbers at the expense of a slight wound. She offers to make him groom of her chamber, but fearful of being recognized, he declines. Finally she lays her fortune at his feet, but he has too much generosity to accept the offer. Leaving a letter revealing his true rank and his poverty, he sails for Persia. Sometime later, the return of Placentia's long lost brother, by depriving her of her fortune, puts her on a level with her lover.

Philidore is captured by pirates and with eleven others set on shore on a desert strand. Three of the little company reach civilization. After recuperating their strength, they set out for Persia overland, but a tiger deprives Philidore of his two companions. A little later he rescues an unknown youth from three assailants, but not before the stranger has been seriously wounded. A passing traveller carries them to the castle of a Persian nobleman. There Philidore waits with the utmost impatience for the wounded man to recover strength enough to relate his story, but this, as also the misfortunes, perplexities, and dangers to which the despairing passion of the enamoured Placentia occasioned her to reduce herself, and the catastrophe of Philidore's surprising fate, must be told in a Second Part.

Part II. The youthful stranger, concealing his name and family, relates the sad effects of his love for the favorite wife of the Bashaw of Liperto, and how by her aid he was enabled to escape from slavery, only to be pursued and about to be retaken by janizaries when rescued by Philidore.

Our hero is kindly received by his uncle in Persia, who soon dies and leaves him sole heir of an enormous fortune. He is now Placentia's equal in wealth as well as rank, and immediately embarks for England. Driven into Baravat by contrary winds, he is moved to ransom a female captive on hearing of her grief at her hard fate, but what is his surprise when the fair slave proves to be Placentia. "Kisses, embraces, and all the fond endearments of rewarded passion made up for their want of speech—in their expressive looks, and eager graspings, the violence of their mutual flame was more plainly demonstrated, than it could have been by the greatest elegance of language—those of the Persians that stood by, who understood not English, easily perceived, not only that they were lovers, but also that they were so to the most unbounded height of tender passion."

Placentia relates how she had eluded her brother and set sail to rejoin her lover, how she had been saved from the arms of the brutal ship's captain by a timely attack of pirates, and how, sold to a Moslem merchant and still annoyed by the attentions of the captain, she had abandoned all thoughts of life till redeemed by Philidore's generosity.

With Placentia, her maid, and young Tradewell, the maid's lover, ransomed, Philidore sails blissfully to England. But upon landing Placentia becomes suddenly cold to him. He forces his way into her house, and finds that her brother is the young stranger whose life he had saved in Persia. Meanwhile Placentia, whose fortune is now no match for Philidore's, flees to parts unknown, leaving a letter conjuring him to forget her. After a long search the brother and lover find her place of concealment, and the former removes her scruples by settling a large estate upon her. "Nothing could be more splendid than the celebration of their nuptials; and of their future bliss, the reader may better judge

GEORGE WHICHER

by their almost unexampled love, their constancy, their generosity and nobleness of soul, than by any description I am able to give of it."

"Philidore and Placentia" is one of the few novels by Mrs. Haywood that do not pretend to a moral purpose. Realism needed some justification, for realism at the time almost invariably meant a picture of vice and folly, and an author could not expose objectionable things except in the hope that they would lessen in fact as they increased in fiction. But in spite of the disapproval sometimes expressed for fables on the ground of their inherent untruth, idealistic romances were generally justified as mirrors of all desirable virtues. Pious Mrs. Penelope Aubin wrote no other kind of fiction, though she sometimes admitted a deep-dyed villain for the sake of showing his condign punishment at the hands of providence. It was perhaps due to the sale of this lady's novels, largely advertised toward the end of 1727 and apparently very successful, that Mrs. Haywood was encouraged to desert her favorite field of exemplary novels showing the dangerous effects of passion for an excursion into pure romance. That she found the attempt neither congenial nor profitable may be inferred from the fact that it was not repeated.

If the highly imaginary romances suffered from an excess of delicacy, certain other tales by Mrs. Haywood overleaped decency as far on the other side. The tendency of fiction before Richardson was not toward refinement. The models, French and Spanish, which writers in England found profit in imitating, racked sensationalism to the utmost degree by stories of horrible and perverted lust. All the excitement that could be obtained from incest, threatened, narrowly averted, or actually committed, was offered to eager readers. Usually, as in Defoe's "Moll Flanders" or Fielding's "Tom Jones," ignorance of birth was an essential element in the plot. A story of this type in which the catastrophe is prevented by a timely discovery of the hero's parentage, is "The Force of Nature: or, the Lucky Disappointment" (1725).

Felisinda, daughter of Don Alvario of Valladolid, falls in love with a dependent of her father's named Fernando, who returns her passion, but when by a dropped letter she reveals their mutual tenderness, her father becomes exceedingly disordered and threatens to marry her out of hand to Don Carlos, who had long solicited the match. That generous lover, however, refuses to marry her against her will. The disappointment proves mortal to Don Alvario, who leaves his estate to Felisinda and Fernando equally, provided they do not marry each other. Felisinda is committed to the care of an abbess named Berinthia, but by the aid of a probationer, Alantha, the lovers manage to correspond. They agree that Fernando shall convert his moiety to ready money, convey it to Brussels, and there await Felisinda, whose escape he entrusts to a friend, Cleomas. Alantha, meantime, has fallen in love with Fernando, and substitutes herself for Felisinda. Cleomas in conducting the supposed mistress of his friend to the nearest port falls under the influence of her beauty and attempts to betray her, but is prevented and slain by a chance passenger, who turns out to be Carlos. He brings Alantha to a better mind, and conducts her in search of Fernando, but they discover in Brussels that he has set out again for Spain. When Fernando reaches Valladolid to inquire what has become of Cleomas and his lady, he is arrested on the charge of abducting Alantha. At the trial he is accused of having made away with her, and is sentenced to death, whereupon Berinthia, the abbess, faints, and being revived, owns him for her son by Alvario, and "in tears and blessings pours out all the mother on him." At the proper moment Carlos comes in with Alantha to prove Fernando's innocence. Felisinda rewards the constancy of Carlos, and Fernando can do no less than marry Alantha.

Incest is almost the only crime not to be found in the extraordinary series of barefaced and infamous intrigues crowded into the pages of "The Injur'd Husband: or, the Mistaken Resentment" (1723). The author naively remarks in the dedication that "The Subject of the Trifle I presume to offer, is, The Worst of Women," and she has indeed out-villained the blackest of her male villains in the character of the wicked Baroness.

The doting Baron de Tortillee marries the lascivious and extravagant Mademoiselle La Motte, who promotes the villainous Du Lache to be the instrument of her vile pleasures. After enjoying several lovers of his procuring, she fixes her affections upon the worthy Beauclair. Du Lache despairs of ensnaring him, because he is about to marry the lovely Montamour, but by a series of base expedients he manages to blacken the character of that lady in her lover's eyes, and to put the charms of the Baroness in such a light that Beauclair is at length drawn in to pay his court to her. For sometime she thus successfully deludes her husband, but when the despicable La Branche openly boasts of her favors and allows some of her letters to fall into the hands of one of her numerous lovers, her perfidy is soon completely exposed. To add to her confusion she hears that the Baron, whom she had drugged into idiocy and sent into the country, has been cured by a skilful physician and is about to return. Du Lache despatches two assassins to murder him on the road, but the Baron by a lucky chance escapes the murderers, forces them to confess, and sets out to punish his guilty wife. Meanwhile Beauclair suspects that he has wronged his innocent lady and endeavors to see her, but she at first refuses to see him, and when by a ruse he gains access to her presence, will not listen to him or give him any grounds for hope. In despair he returns to Paris and meets the young Vrayment. He discovers the infamous Du Lache hiding in a convent. To save his life the wretch offers to reveal the frauds he had put in practice against Montamour, but while he is doing so, the Baron meets them, and concluding that Beauclair is in collusion with the villain, attacks them both. Beauclair disarms his antagonist and is about to return him his weapon, when Du Lache stabs the Baron in the back. Vrayment has witnessed the quarrel and summoned assistance. Beauclair and Du Lache are haled before a magistrate and are about to be condemned equally for the crime, when Vrayment reveals herself as Montamour disguised as a man, and persuades the judge that Beauclair is innocent. Du Lache and his accomplices are broken on the wheel, the Baroness takes poison, and Beauclair is united to his faithful Montamour.

In the conduct of the story the writer shows no deficiency in expressing the passions, but rather a want of measure, for thrill follows thrill so fast that the reader can hardly realize what is happening. And as if the lusts and crimes of the Baroness did not furnish enough sensational incidents, the tender romance of Beauclair and Montamour is superadded. The hero is a common romantic type, easily inconstant, but rewarded above his merits by a faithful mistress. A woman disguised as a man was a favorite device with Mrs. Haywood as well as with other writers of love stories, but one need read only the brazen Mrs. Charke's memoirs or Defoe's realistic "Moll Flanders" to discover that it was a device not unheard of in real life. The actual occurrence of such disguises, however, made no difference to the female writers of fiction. Anything soul-stirring, whether from romances or from plays, was equally grist to their mills.

In seeking for the most dramatic *dénouements* sensational romancers were not long in perceiving the suspense that could be produced by involving the chief characters in a trial for their lives. Mrs. Behn had by that means considerably protracted the interest in "The Fair Jilt: or, the Amours of Prince Tarquin and Miranda" (1688), and Mrs. Haywood, following her example, succeeded in giving a last stimulus to the jaded nerves of the readers of "The Force of Nature" and "The Injur'd Husband." And finally the title-page of an anonymous work attributed to her indicates that the struggling authoress was not insensible to the popular demand for romances of roguery. A prospective buyer might have imagined that he was securing a criminal biography in "Memoirs of the Baron de Brosse, Who was Broke on the Wheel in the Reign of Lewis XIV Containing, An Account of his Amours. With Several Particulars relating to the Wars in those Times," but the promise of the title was unfulfilled, for Mrs. Haywood was no journalist to make capital out of a malefactor's exit from the world. The whole book is a chronicle of the Baron's unsuccessful pursuit of a hard-hearted beauty named Larissa, mingled with little histories of the Baron's rivals, of a languishing Madam de Monbray, and of Larissa's mother. The fair charmer finally marries a count, and her lover, plunged into adequate despair, can barely exert himself to answer a false accusation trumped up by the revengeful Monbray. With the verdict in his favor the story ends abruptly, and the promised continuation was apparently never written. We read nothing of the wars, nor of the Baron's execution on the wheel.

Tortures, tragedies of blood, and heinous crimes added piquancy to Mrs. Haywood's love stories, but were not the normal material of her romances. Her talent was chiefly for "soft things." She preferred the novel of intrigue and passion in which the characters could be run through a breathless maze of amatory adventures, with a pause now and again to relate a digressive episode for variety's sake. Typical of this sort, the best adapted to the romancer's genius, is "The Agreeable Caledonian: or, Memoirs of Signiora di Morella, a Roman Lady, Who made her Escape from a Monastery at Viterbo, for the Love of a Scots Nobleman. Intermix'd with many other Entertaining little Histories and Adventures which presented themselves to her in the Course of her Travels." No moralizing, no romantic idealism disturbs the rapid current of events. It is a pure "cloak and sword" novel, definitely located in Italy, with all the machinery of secret assignations, escapes from convents, adventures on the road and at inns, sudden assaults, duels, seductions, and revenge characteristic of Spanish fiction.

Don Jaques di Morella determines to marry his daughter, Clementina, to a certain Cardinal, who has offered to renounce the scarlet hat for love of her. When she piques her lover by her evident unwillingness to wed, Don Jaques packs her off to a convent at Viterbo. By picking up a copy of verses Clementina becomes acquainted with Signiora Miramene, who relates the history of her correspondence with the Baron Glencairn.

Clementina becomes the instrument of the lovers, but no sooner sees the lovely North Briton than she herself is captivated. In response to her proffered affection, Glencairn manages by an extraordinary device to convey her out of the convent. In spite of the rage of Dan Jaques they escape to Sienna. The further surprising turns in their affairs to be later communicated to the public.

Part II. At Sienna the lovers enjoy a season of perfect felicity until Don Jaques comes to town in pursuit of a defaulting steward, discovers Clementina, and apprehends the pair. While the two are confined in separate convents awaiting trial, Clementina's maid, Ismenia (who has already related her little history), becomes their go-between and serves her mistress the same trick that Clementina had already played upon her friend Miramene. Ismenia and the faithless Baron decamp to parts unknown, while Clementina's father starts back to Rome with his recreant daughter. In man's clothes she escapes from her parent to seek revenge upon her lover. At an inn she hears a woman in the next room complaining of her gallant's desertion, and going in to console her, hears the moving story of Signiora Vicino and Monsieur Beaumont, told as a warning to the credulous and unwary sex. The injured fair enters a convent.

Still in pursuit of her lover, Clementina on Montelupe meets the funeral of a young woman who had been torn to pieces by wolves. The chief mourner proves to be Glencairn. She is hindered in an attempt to stab him and thrown into prison, where he visits her and disarms her resentment by offering to marry her. After the ceremony they proceed to Paris where each plunges into dissipation. Finally they separate, Clementina dies of a fever, and the Baron is left free to pursue his inclinations through a possible third part, which, however, was never written.

After a slumber of forty years "The Agreeable Caledonian" was reprinted, as the "Monthly Review" informs us, from a copy corrected by Mrs. Haywood not long before her death.[16] The review continues, "It is like the rest of Mrs. Haywood's novels, written in a tawdry style, now utterly exploded; the romances of these days being reduced much nearer the standard of nature, and to the manners of the living world."

---

16. *Monthly Review*, XXXVIII, 412, May, 1768. *Clementina; or the History of an Italian Lady, who made her Escape from a Monastery*, etc.

Realism is, indeed, far to seek in the brief but intricate tissue of incidents that made the novel of 1728. To a taste accustomed to "Sir Charles Grandison," and "Peregrine Pickle," and "The Sentimental Journey" the rehash of Eliza Haywood's novel must have seemed very far even from the manners of the world of fiction. The judgment of the "Critical Review" was still more savage in its accuracy.[17] "This is a republication of a dull, profligate Haywoodian production, in which all the males are rogues, and all the females whores, without a glimpse of plot, fable, or sentiment." In its uncompromising literalness the critic's verdict ranks with the learned Ascham's opinion of the "Morte D'Arthur,"—except that it has not been superseded. The same animadversion might be urged against Defoe's "Colonel Jacque" or "The Fortunate Mistress." If Mrs. Haywood sinned against the standards of the age to come, she was not out of touch with the spirit of her own generation.

As a writer she knew but one unfailing recipe for popularity: whatever she touched must be forthwith gilded with passion. The chief *raison d'être* for "The Fair Hebrew: or, a True, but Secret History of Two Jewish Ladies, Who lately resided in London" (1729) was to gratify the prejudices of anti-Semitic readers, yet it is hardly distinguishable from her sentimental love stories.

The young and gay Dorante, going to the synagogue for a lark, is tempted by the sight of a fair hand to break into the woman's apartment and to expose himself to the charms of the beautiful Kesiah. He engages her in a correspondence, but at their first interview she gives him clearly to understand that he can gain nothing from her but by marriage. Driven by his unhappy passion, he complies with her demand, and she becomes a Church of England woman. But once married, Kesiah is too proud to permit the concealment that prudence demands. Though his father is sure to disinherit them, she insists upon revealing the marriage.

Dorante entrusts his small stock of money to his wife's brother, Abimelech, in order to start him in trade. The Jew goes to Holland with a woman whom he has saved from religious murder at the hands of a Levite, and nothing further is heard from him or the money. Imprisoned by his creditors, Dorante is persuaded by his wife to sign away the entail of his estate in return for a sum of money. Thereupon she departs with the gold and a new gallant, leaving her unhappy husband to be rescued from want by the kindness, of a younger brother. After the poor solace

---

17. *Critical Review*, XXV, 59.

of hearing that Kesiah and her paramour have been lost at sea, he dies of a broken heart.[18]

Though Eliza Haywood exhausted nearly every possible bit of sensationalism that could be extracted from tales of passion, she almost never made use of the heroic feats of arms which constituted a no less important resource of the French romances. Her heroes are victors in love but not in war. The sole exception is a little romance of Moorish chivalry in the eighth century. Though this period had already been pre-empted by Mrs. Manley's "Memoirs of Europe," there is little doubt that Mrs. Haywood was responsible for "The Arragonian Queen: A Secret History" (1724), a peculiar blend of heroic adventures in battle, bullfight, and tournament, with amorous intrigues of the most involved kind.

Prince Albaraizor of Arragon goes to assist Omar, King of Valencia, against a traitorous foe, and with the help of the young general, Abdelhamar, succeeds in vanquishing the enemy, though the latter youth is seriously wounded while performing miracles of valor. To reward the conqueror the hand of the Princess Zephalinda is bestowed upon him, but she unfortunately is already enamored of Abdelhamar, whom she had learned to love at a bullfight. But in spite of a repining letter from her constant lover, and in spite of his appearance before her all pale and trembling from his wounds, the Princess refuses to deviate from her duty.

> "The next Day the Marriage was celebrated with all the intended Magnificence, and on their return from the Mosque, the Prince and Princess repair'd to a stately Scaffold, adorn'd with inventive Luxury, whence they might behold a Tournament, the Prize of which was a Sword richly embellish'd with Diamonds, to be given by the Princess to him that should overcome; the whole Court were there, endeavouring to outshine each other in the Costliness of their Apparel—within the Barriers were all the Flower of the adjoining Kingdoms, drawn thither with a Thirst of Fame, and a Desire to shew their Dexterity. The Arragonian Noblemen were the Defenders against all Comers, and were like to have carried away the Prize, behaving themselves with the utmost

---

18. In both editions is advertised "Persecuted Virtue: or, the Cruel Lover. A True Secret History, Writ at the Request of a Lady of Quality," which was advertised also in the *Daily Post*, 28 Nov. 1728. I have not found a copy.

Skill and Courage, when there appear'd in the Lists a Knight in black Armour, whose whole Air and dexterity in Horsemanship immediately attracted the Eyes of the numerous Spectators; the first Course he made, confirm'd them in the good opinion they had conceiv'd of him: in short, no body was able to stand against him, and he remain'd Conqueror, with the universal Applause of the whole Company.—He waited for sometime, to see if no fresh Challengers would offer themselves; but none appearing, he was led to the Princess's Scaffold, to receive the Reward he had so well merited: He took it with the greatest Submission, but without putting up his Beaver, or discovering who he was, and kissing it with profound Respect, retir'd, without so much as making any obeisance to the King or Prince; and mixing himself with the Crowd of Knights, got off without being discover'd. Everybody was surpriz'd at the uncourteous Behaviour of so otherwise accomplish'd a Cavalier, but none could possibly give the least guess at who it should be—the succeeding Diversions soon put him out of everybody's Thoughts but Zephalinda's; she well knew it could be none but Abdelhamar, and trembled lest he should have been discovered, fearing his concealing his Recovery, and his disrespectful Carriage towards her Father and her Husband, might have given room to Surmises prejudicial to her Honour: but when watching him with her Eyes, and seeing him get off unfollow'd, or observ'd, she then began afresh to pine at Fate, who could render Abdelhamar Conqueror in every Action that he undertook, and only vanquish'd when he fought in hopes of gaining her."

The Prince and his bride return to their own country to receive the crown. By the most tender assiduities Albaraizor has almost succeeded in gaining the love of his wife when Abdelhamar again intrudes as ambassador to congratulate him on his coronation. Though her old love returns more strongly than ever, the Queen guards her honor well, and insists that her lover marry Selyma, a captive Princess. But that lady, stung by Abdelhamar's indifference, learns to hate him, and out of revenge persuades the King that his wife is unfaithful to him. An indiscreet letter from Abdelhamar confirms his suspicions. He orders both Queen and ambassador cast into prison and by his woes destroys the happiness of the whole court.

The passages relating the monarch's love and jealousy are described with a fulness entirely lacking in the tournament scene quoted above, and we may fairly infer that both writer and reader were more deeply interested in affairs of the heart than in feats of arms, however glorious. The emphasis given to love rather than to war in this tale is significant as a contrast to the opposite tendency in such romances of a century later as "Ivanhoe," in which a tournament scene very similar in outline to that in "The Arragonian Queen" is told with the greatest attention to warlike detail, while the love story, though not allowed to languish, is kept distinctly subordinate to the narrative of chivalric adventure. Mrs. Haywood, however, was too warm-blooded a creature to put aside the interests of the heart for the sake of a barbarous Gothic brawl, and too experienced a writer not to know that her greatest forte lay in painting the tender rather than the sterner passions.

In this respect she forms a decided contrast to Defoe, whose men and women are almost never startled out of their matter-of-fact attitude. His picaresque characters, though outwardly rogues or their female counterparts, have at bottom something of the dissenting parson and cool-headed, middle-aged man of business. Whatever else they may be, they are never love-sick. Passion is to them a questionable asset, and if they marry, they are like to have the matter over with in the course of half a paragraph. Eliza Haywood, however, possessed in excess the one gift that Defoe lacked. To the scribbling authoress love was the force that motivated all the world. Crude and conventional as are many of her repeated attempts to analyze the workings of a mind under the sway of soft desires, she nevertheless succeeded now and then in actuating her heroines with genuine emotion. Both romance and realism were woven into the intricate web of the Richardsonian novel, and the contribution of Mrs. Haywood deserves to be remembered if only because she supplied the one element missing in Defoe's masterpieces. Each writer in his day was considered paramount in his or her particular field.[19]

---

19. An anonymous poem prefixed to Mrs. Elizabeth Boyd's *The Happy Unfortunate; or, the Female Page* (1737) testifies to Mrs. Haywood's reputation in the following terms:

> "Yeild (sic) Heywood yeild, yeild all whose tender Strains,
> Inspire the Dreams of Maids and lovesick Swains;
> Who taint the unripen'd Girl with amorous Fire,
> And hint the first faint Dawnings of Desire:
> Wing each Love-Atom, that in Embryo lies,
> And teach young Parthenissa's Breasts to rise.
> A new Elisa writes," etc., etc.

III

The Duncan Campbell Pamphlets

Only once did Eliza Haywood compete with Defoe upon the same ground. Both novelists were alive to the value of sensational matter, but as we have seen, appealed to the reader's emotional nature from different sides. Defoe with his strong interest in practical life looked for stirring incidents, for strange and surprising adventures on land and sea, for unusual or uncanny occurrences; whereas Mrs. Haywood, less a journalist than a romancer, rested her claim to public favor upon the secure basis of the tender passions. In the books exploiting the deaf and dumb prophet Duncan Campbell, whose fame, once illustrated by notices in the "Tatler" and "Spectator,"[1] was becoming a little dimmed by 1720, each writer chose the kind of material that the natural propensity and previous experience of each had trained him or her to use with the greatest success.

Accordingly the "History of the Life and Adventures of Mr. Duncan Campbell, a gentleman who, though deaf and dumb, writes down any stranger's name at first sight, with their future contingencies of fortune: Now living in Exeter Court, over against the Savoy in the Strand," published by Curll on 30 April, 1720, and written largely by Defoe, devoted only four chapters directly to the narrative of the conjuror's life, while four chapters and the Appendix were given over to disquisitions upon the method of teaching deaf and dumb persons to read and write; upon the perception of demons, genii, or familiar spirits; upon the second sight; upon magic in all its branches; and upon the laws against false diviners and soothsayers. Beside showing the keenness of his interest in the supernatural, the author deliberately avoided any occasion for talking gossip or for indulging "persons of airy tempers" with sentimental love-tales. "Instead of making them a bill of fare out of patchwork romances and polluting scandal," reads the preface signed by Duncan Campbell, "the good old gentleman who wrote the adventures of my life has made it his business to treat them with a great variety of entertaining passages which always terminate in

---

1. *Tatler*, No. 14; *Spectator*, Nos. 323, 474, 560.

morals that tend to the edification of all readers, of whatsoever sex, age, or profession." Those who came to consult the seer on affairs of the heart, therefore, received only the scantiest mention from his biographer, and never were the languishing and sighing of Mr. Campbell's devotees described with any romantic glamor. On the contrary, Defoe portrayed in terse and homely phrases the follies and affectations of the dumb man's fair clients. The young blooming beauty who found little Duncan "wallowing in the dust" and bribed him with a sugarplum to reveal the name of her future husband; the "sempstress with an itching desire for a parson"; housekeepers in search of stolen goods; the "widow who bounced" from one end of the room to the other and finally "scuttled too airily downstairs for a woman in her clothes"; and the chambermaid disguised as a fine lady, who by "the toss of her head, the jut of the bum, the sidelong leer of the eye" proclaimed her real condition—these types are treated by Defoe in a blunt realistic manner entirely foreign to Eliza Haywood's vein. Some passages,[2] perhaps, by a sentiment too exalted or by a description in romantic style suggest the hand of another writer, possibly Mrs. Haywood, but more probably William Bond, in whose name the reprint of 1728 was issued.[3] But in the main, the book reflected Defoe's strong tendency to speculate upon unusual and supernatural phenomena, and utterly failed to "divulge the secret intrigues and amours of one part of the sex, to give the other part room to make favorite scandal the subject of their discourse."[4]

2. Particularly the incongruous description of Duncan Campbell's first appearance in London, where the writer finds the "heavenly youth" seated like a young Adonis in the "center of an angelic tribe" of "the most beautiful females that ever my eyes beheld," etc. G.A. Aitken's edition of *The Life and Adventures of Mr. Duncan Campbell*, 87–9.

3. *The Supernatural Philosopher* . . . by William Bond, of Bury St. Edmonds, Suffolk. The preface signed by Campbell to Defoe's *Life and Adventures* states that the book was revised by "a young gentleman of my acquaintance." Professor Trent, however, includes Mrs. Haywood with Bond as a possible assistant in the revision. See *The Cambridge History of English Literature*, IX, 23.

4. Neither Defoe nor Mrs. Haywood contributed to the little budget of miscellaneous matter prefixed to the second issue of the *Life and Adventures* (August, 1720) and sometimes found separately under the title: *Mr. Campbell's Pacquet, for the Entertainment of Gentlemen and Ladies. Containing I Verses to Mr. Campbell, Occasioned by the History of his Life and Adventures. By Mrs. Fowke, Mr. Philips, &c. II. The Parallel, a Poem. Comparing the Poetical Productions of Mr. Pope, with the Prophetical Predictions of Mr. Campbell. By Capt. Stanhope*, (i. e. W. Bond.) *III. An Account of a most surprizing Apparition; sent from Launceston in Cornwall. Attested by the Rev. Mr. Ruddie, Minister there.* London: For T. Bickerton. 1720. See W. Lee, *Daniel Defoe*, 322–8.

That Defoe had refrained from treating one important aspect of Duncan Campbell's activities he was well aware. "If I was to tell his adventures with regard, for instance, to women that came to consult him, I might, perhaps, have not only written the stories of eleven thousand virgins that died maids, but have had the relations to give of as many married women and widows, and the work would have been endless."[5] In his biography of the Scotch prophet he does not propose to clog the reader with any adventures save the most remarkable and those in various ways mysterious.

The "method of swelling distorted and commented trifles into volumes" he is content to leave to the writers of fable and romance. It was not long before the press-agents of the dumb presager found a romancer willing to undertake the task that Defoe neglected. Mrs. Haywood in her association with Aaron Hill and his circle could hardly have escaped knowing William Bond, who in 1724 was playing Steele to Hill's Addison in producing the numbers of the "Plain Dealer." Instigated perhaps by him, the rising young novelist contributed on 19 March, 1724, the second considerable work on the fortune-teller, under the caption: "A Spy upon the Conjurer: or, a Collection of Surprising Stories, with Names, Places, and particular Circumstances relating to Mr. Duncan Campbell, commonly known by the Name of the Deaf and Dumb Man; and the astonishing Penetration and Event of his Predictions. Written to my Lord—— by a Lady, who for more than Twenty Years past; has made it her Business to observe all Transactions in the Life and Conversation of Mr. Campbell."[6]

"As long as Atalantis shall be read," some readers were sure to find little to their taste in the curious information contained in the first biography of Campbell, but Mrs. Haywood was not reluctant to gratify an appetite for scandal when she could profitably cater to it. Developing the clue afforded her by the announcement in Defoe's "Life and Adventures" of a forthcoming little pocket volume of original letters that passed between Mr. Campbell and his correspondents,[7] she composed a number of epistles as coming from all sorts of applicants

---

5. *Life and Adventures of Mr. Duncan Campbell*, 171.

6. This volume was announced in the *British Journal* as early as Dec. 15, 1722.

7. She or Bond may have inserted the passage to advertise a projected work. Mr. Spectator had already remarked of the letters that came to his office: "I know some Authors, who would pick up a *Secret History* out of such materials, and make a Bookseller an Alderman by the Copy." (No. 619.)

to the prophet. These missives, however, were preceded by a long letter addressed to an anonymous lord and signed "Justicia," which was chiefly concocted of anecdotes illustrative of the dumb man's powers. Unlike the incidents in Defoe's work, the greater number of the stories relate to love affairs in the course of which one party or the other invoked the seer's assistance. Although the author was thoroughly acquainted with the previous history of Mr. Campbell,[8] she was evidently more interested in the phenomena of passion than in the theory of divination, A brief discussion of astrology, witchcraft, and dreams easily led her to a narrative of "Mr. Campbell's sincerity exemplify'd, in the story of a lady injured in the tenderest part by a pretended friend." A glance through the table of contents reveals the preponderance of such headings as "A strange story of a young lady, who came to ask the name of her husband"; "A whimsical story of an old lady who wanted a husband"; "Reflections on the inconstancy of men. A proof of it in a ruin'd girl, that came to ask Mr. Campbell's advice"; "A story of my Lady Love-Puppy"; "A merry story of a lady's chamber-maid, cook-maid, and coach-man," and so on. Evidences of an attempt to suggest, if not actual references to, contemporary scandal, are to be found in such items as "A strange instance of vanity and jealousy in the behaviour of Mrs. F——"; "The particulars of the fate of Mrs. J—— L—— "; and "A story of the Duke of—— 's mistress." It is not surprising that "Memoirs of a Certain Island" appeared within six months of "A Spy upon the Conjurer."

When "Justicia" refers to her personal relations with the lord to whom her letter is addressed, her comments are still more in keeping with the acknowledged forte of the lady novelist. They are permeated with the tenderest emotions. The author of "Moll Flanders" and "The Fortunate Mistress" might moralize upon the unhappy consequences of love, but he was inclined to regard passion with an equal mind. He stated facts simply. Love, in his opinion, was not a strong motive when uncombined with interest. But Eliza Haywood held the romantic watchword of all for love, and her books are a continual illustration of *Amor vincit omnia*. In the present case her words seem to indicate that the passions of love and jealousy so often experienced by her characters were not unfamiliar to her own breast. Even Duncan Campbell's predictions were unable to alter her destiny.

---

8. Defoe's *Life and Adventures* is mentioned on pp. 17 (with a quotation), 61, 111, 246, 257.

"But tho' I was far enough from disbelieving what he said, yet Youth, Passion, and Inadvertency render'd his Cautions ineffectual. It was in his Hand-Writing I first beheld the dear fatal Name, which has since been the utter Destruction of my Peace: It was from him I knew I should be undone by Love and the Perfidy of Mankind, before I had the least Notion of the one, or had seen any of the other charming enough to give me either Pain or Pleasure. . . Yet besotted as I was, I had neither the Power of defending myself from the Assaults of Love, nor Thought sufficient to enable me to make those Preparations which were necessary for my future Support, while I had yet the means" . . . (p. 13).

"Yet so it is with our inconsiderate Sex!—To vent a present Passion,—for the short liv'd Ease of railing at the Baseness of an ungrateful Lover,—to gain a little Pity,—we proclaim our Folly, and become the Jest of all who know us.—A forsaken Woman immediately grows the Object of Derision,—rallied by the Men, and pointed at by every little Flirt, who fancies herself secure in her own Charms of never being so, and thinks 'tis want of Merit only makes a Wretch.

"For my dear Lord, I am sensible, tho' our Wounds have been a long time heal'd, there yet remains a Tenderness, which, if touch'd, will smart afresh.—The Darts of Passion, such as we have felt, make too indeliable an Impression ever to be quite eraz'd;—they are not content with the eternal Sear they leave on the Reputation. . ." (p.76).

These passages are in substance and style after Eliza Haywood's manner, while the experiences therein hinted at do not differ essentially from the circumstances of her own life.

The various aspects of love and jealousy are also the theme of the second and third parts of "A Spy upon the Conjurer."[9] The two packets of letters were merely imaginary, unless the pseudonymous signatures of some of the missives may have aided contemporary readers to "smoke"

---

9. Part II. Being a Collection of Letters found in Mr. Campbell's Closet. By the Lady who wrote the foregoing sheets. Part III. Containing some Letters from Persons of Mr. Campbell's more particular Acquaintance.

GEORGE WHICHER

allusions to current gossip. At any rate the references are now happily beyond our power to fathom.

Apparently the taste for Duncan Campbell anecdotes was stimulated by the piquant sauce of scandal, for beside the several issues of "A Spy upon the Conjurer" a second and smaller volume of the same sort was published on 10 May, 1725. This sixpenny pamphlet of forty pages, entitled "The Dumb Projector: Being a Surprizing Account of a Trip to Holland made by Mr. Duncan Campbell. With the Manner of his Reception and Behaviour there. As also the various and diverting Occurrences that happened on his Departure," was, like the former work, couched in the form of a letter to a nobleman and signed "Justicia." Both from internal evidence[10] and from the style it can be assigned with confidence to the author of "A Spy upon the Conjurer." The story, relating how Mr. Campbell was induced to go into Holland in the hope of making his fortune, how he was disappointed, the extraordinary instances of his power, and his adventures amatory and otherwise, is of little importance as a narrative. The account differs widely from that of Campbell's trip to the Netherlands in the "Life and Adventures" of 1720.

Soon after the publication of "The Dumb Projector" Defoe also made a second contribution to the now considerable Duncan Campbell literature under the title of "The Friendly Daemon: or, the Generous Apparition. Being a True Narrative of a Miraculous Cure newly performed upon. . . Dr. Duncan Campbell, by a familiar Spirit, that appeared to him in a white surplice, like a Cathedral Singing Boy." The quotation of the story from Glanvil already used by the prophet's original biographer, and the keen interest in questions of the supernatural displayed by the writer, make the attribution of this piece to Defoe a practical certainty. Evidently, then, Eliza Haywood was not the only one to profit by keeping alive the celebrity of the fortune-teller.

---

10. "The Pleasure with which you received my *Spy* on the Conjurer, encourages me to offer you a little Supplement to it, having since my finishing that Book, had the opportunity of discovering something concerning Mr. Campbell, which I believe your Lordship will allow to be infinitely more surprizing than anything I have yet related." *The Dumb Projector*, 5. Mr. G. A. Aitken, in his introduction to Defoe's *Life and Adventures*, gives the two pieces unhesitatingly to Mrs. Haywood, while other students of Defoe,— Leslie Stephen, Lee, Wright, and Professor Trent,—are unanimous in their opinion that the first exploiter of the dumb wizard could have had no hand in the writing of these amplifications. The latest bibliographer of romances and tales, Mr. Arundell Esdaile, however, follows the B.M. catalogue in listing *The Dumb Projector* under the convenient name of Defoe.

The year 1728 was marked by the reissue of the "Life and Adventures" as "The Supernatural Philosopher. . . by William Bond," whose probable connection with the work has already been discussed, and by the publication in the "Craftsman"[11] of a letter, signed "Fidelia," describing a visit to Duncan Campbell. The writer, who professes an intense admiration for Mr. Caleb D'Anvers and all his works, relates how the dumb oracle, after writing down her name, had prophesied that the Craftsman would certainly gain his point in 1729. She concludes with praise of Mr. Campbell, and an offer to conduct Caleb to visit him on the ensuing Saturday. That the communication was not to be regarded as a companion-piece to the letter from Dulcibela Thankley in the "Spectator" (No. 474), was the purport of the editorial statement which introduced it: "I shall make no other Apology for the Vanity, which I may seem guilty of in publishing the following Letter, than assuring the Reader it is *genuine*, and that I do it in Complyance with the repeated Importunity of a *fair Correspondent*." The style of the letter does not strongly suggest that of "A Spy upon the Conjurer," though the concluding sentence, "*Love* shall be there too, who waits forever upon *Wit*," is a sentiment after Eliza's heart. And moreover, though "Fidelia" and "Justicia" may be one and the same persons, Mr. D'Anvers' assurances that the letter is genuine are not to be relied upon with too much confidence, for had he wished to praise himself, he would naturally have resorted to some such device.

The last volume relating to the Scotch wizard did not appear until 1732, two years after Campbell's death. "Secret Memoirs of the late Mr. Duncan Campbel, The famous Deaf and Dumb Gentleman. Written by Himself, who ordered they should be publish'd after his Decease," consisted of 164 pages devoted to miscellaneous anecdotes of the prophet, a reprint of Defoe's "Friendly Daemon" (p. 166), "Original Letters sent to Mr. Campbel by his Consulters" (p. 196), and "An Appendix, By Way of Vindication of Mr. Duncan Campbel, Against That groundless Aspersion cast upon him, That he but pretended to be Deaf and Dumb. By a Friend of the Deceased" (p. 225). The authorship of this book has received but slight attention from students of Defoe, and still remains something of a puzzle. No external evidence on the point has yet come to light, but some probable conclusions may be reached through an examination of the substance and style.

---

11. No. 125, Saturday. 23 November, 1728.

In the first place, there is no probability—the statement on the title-page notwithstanding—that Mr. Campbell himself had anything to do with the composition of the "Memoirs." Since the magician had taken no part in the literary exploitation of his fame during his lifetime, it is fair to infer that he did not begin to do so two years after his death. Moreover, each of the three writers, Bond, Defoe, and Eliza Haywood, already identified with the Campbell pamphlets was perfectly capable of passing off fiction as feigned biography. Both the author of "Memoirs of a Cavalier" and the scribbler of secret histories had repeatedly used the device. There is no evidence, however, that William Bond had any connection with the present work, but a large share of it was almost certainly done by Defoe and Mrs. Haywood.

The former had died full of years on 26 April, 1731, about a year before the "Secret Memoirs" was published. It is possible, however, that he may have assembled most of the material for the book and composed a number of pages. The inclusion of his "Friendly Daemon" makes this suspicion not unlikely. And furthermore, certain anecdotes told in the first section, particularly in the first eighty pages, are such stories as would have appealed to Defoe's penchant for the uncanny, and might well have been selected by him. The style is not different from that of pieces known to be his.

But that the author of "Robinson Crusoe" would have told the "little History" of the young woman without a fortune who obtains the husband she desires by means of a magic cake (p. 86) is scarcely probable, for the story is a sentimental tale that would have appealed to love-sick Lydia Languishes. As far as we know, Defoe remained hard-headed to the last. But Mrs. Haywood when she was not a scandal-monger, was a sentimentalist. The story would have suited her temperament and the tastes of her readers. It is told so much in her manner that one could swear that the originator of the anecdote was *aut Eliza, aut diabola*. A few pages further on (p. 104) appears the incident of a swaggerer who enters the royal vault of Westminster Abbey at dead of night on a wager, and having the tail of his coat twitched by the knife he has stuck in the ground, is frightened into a faint—a story which Mrs. Haywood later retold in different words in her "Female Spectator."[12] The "Secret Memoirs" further informs us by a casual remark of Mr. Campbell's that Eliza Haywood was well acquainted with the seer.

---

12. *The Female Spectator*, 1745, II, 246.

"Sometimes, when surrounded by my Friends, such as Anthony Hammond, Esq; Mr. Philip Horneck, Mr. Philips, Mr.——, Mrs. Centlivre, Mrs. Fowk, Mrs. Eliza Haywood, and other celebrated Wits, of which my House, for some Years has been the general Rendezvous, a good Bowl of Punch before me, and the Glass going round in a constant Circle of Mirth and Good Humour, I have, in a Moment, beheld Sights which has froze my very Blood, and put me into Agonies that disordered the whole Company" (p. 131).

The last anecdote in the first section is a repetition at some length of the story of Campbell's adventures in Holland, not as related in Defoe's "Life and Adventures," but according to the version in Mrs Haywood's "Dumb Projector." The beginning, which has to do with a grave old gentleman who was bit by a viper, is told in almost the same words; indeed some letters that passed between the characters are identically the same, and the end, though much abbreviated, contains a number of sentences taken word for word from the earlier telling of the story. Finally, Mrs. Haywood was the first and hitherto the only writer of the Campbell pamphlets who had printed letters supposedly addressed to the prophet by his clients. The device was peculiarly hers. The "Original Letters sent to Mr. Campbel by his Consulters" in the "Secret Memoirs" are similar to those already composed by her for "A Spy upon the Conjurer." There is no reason to think that she did not invent the later epistles as well as the former.

If, then, a number of anecdotes in the "Secret Memoirs" are suggestive of Mrs. Haywood's known writings, and if one of them remained in her memory thirteen years later; if the pamphlet carefully alludes to Eliza Haywood as one of the dumb seer's particular friends, and if it repeats in slightly different form her peculiar account of the dumb projector's journey into Holland; and if, finally, the book contains a series of letters to Campbell from fictitious correspondents fashioned on the last already used by her, we may conclude that in all likelihood the authoress whose name had previously been associated with Duncan Campbell literature was again concerned in writing or revising this latest work. At least a cautious critic can say that there is no inherent improbability in the theory that Defoe with journalistic instinct, thinking that Campbell's death in 1730 might stimulate public interest in the wizard, had drafted in the rough the manuscript of a new biography, but was prevented by the troubles of his last days from completing it; that after his death the manuscript fell into the hands of Mrs. Haywood, or perhaps was given to her by the publishers Millan and Chrichley to finish; that she revised the material already written, supplemented it with new and old matter of her own, composed a packet of Original Letters, and sent the volume to press. The origin of the "Appendix, by Way of Vindication of Mr. Duncan Campbel" remains unknown, and any theory about the authorship of the "Secret Memoirs" must be regarded in last analysis as largely conjectural.[13]

Though the author of the original "Life and Adventures" has received most of the credit due to Campbell's biographer, Mrs. Haywood, as we have seen, was not less active in exploiting the deaf and dumb gentleman. Her "Spy upon the Conjurer" was fubbed off upon the public as often as Defoe's earlier volume, and neither writer could claim any advantage over the other from his second and slighter contribution. Each held successfully his own coign of vantage. Eliza Haywood, in contemporary opinion, outranked Defoe almost as far as an interpreter of the heart as he surpassed her in concocting an account of a new marvel or a tale of strange adventure. The arbitress of the passions indeed wrote nothing to compare in popularity with "Robinson Crusoe," but before 1740 her "Love in Excess" ran through as many editions as "Moll Flanders" and its abridgments, while "Idalia: or, the Unfortunate Mistress" had been reprinted three times separately and twice with her collected novels before a reissue of Defoe's "Fortunate Mistress" was undertaken. When in 1740 Applebee published a new edition of "Roxana," he had it supplemented by "a continuation of nearly one hundred and fifty pages, many of which are filled with rubbish about women named Cleomira and Belinda."[14] Here again Mrs. Haywood's red herring crossed the trail of Defoe, for oddly enough the sheets thus accurately characterized were transcribed word for word from Eliza's second novel, "The British Recluse." At the point where the heroine swallows a sleeping potion supposing it poison, faints, and is thought to be dead, the narrative breaks off abruptly with the words:

---

13. In 1734 appeared a compilation of tables for computing Easter, etc., entitled *Time's Telescope Universal and Perpetual, Fitted for all Countries and Capacities . . . By Duncan Campbell*. What connection, if any, this book had with the fortune-teller or with any of the persons connected with his biography appears not to have been determined.

14. G.A. Aitken, Introduction to *The Fortunate Mistress*, viii.

"Though the History of Cleomira and Belinda's Misfortunes, may be thought foreign to my Affairs. . . yet it is absolutely necessary I should give it a Place, because it is the Source, or Spring, of many strange and uncommon Scenes, which happened to me during the remaining Part of my Life, and which I cannot give an Account of without". . .[15]

The pages which follow relate how Roxana became reconciled to her daughter, died in peace, and was buried at Hornsey. The curious reader finds, however, no further mention of Belinda and her friend. Evidently Applebee's hack simply stole as much copy as he needed from an almost forgotten book, trusting to receive his money before the fraud was discovered. The volumes of Eliza Haywood were indeed a mine of emotional scenes, and those who wished to read of warm desires or palpitating passions had to turn to her romances or do without. Wretched as her work seems in comparison to the modern novel, it was for the time being the nearest approach to idealistic fiction and to the analysis of human feelings. Defoe's romances of incident were the triumphant culmination of the picaresque type; Mrs. Haywood's sentimental tales were in many respects mere vague inchoations of a form as yet to be produced. But when freed from the impurities of intrigue and from the taint of scandal, the novel of heart interest became the dominant type of English fiction. Unfortunately, however, Eliza Haywood was too practical a writer to outrun her generation. The success of "A Spy upon the Conjurer" may have convinced her that a ready market awaited stories of amorous adventure and hinted libel. At any rate, she soon set out to gratify the craving for books of that nature in a series of writings which redounded little to her credit, though they brought her wide notoriety.

---

15. *The Fortunate Mistress; or, a History of the Life and Vast Variety of Fortunes of Mademoiselle de Beleau* . . . London: Printed for E. Applebee. 1740. p. 359. Pp. 300–59 are taken from *The British Recluse*.

GEORGE WHICHER

IV

SECRET HISTORIES AND SCANDAL NOVELS

S ome tentative experiments in the way of scandal-mongering may be found in Mrs. Haywood's work even before the first of her Duncan Campbell pamphlets. Many of the short romances discussed in the second chapter were described on the title-page as secret histories, while others apparently indistinguishable from them in kind were denominated novels. "Love in Excess" and "The Unequal Conflict," for instance, were given the latter title, but a tale like "Fantomina," evidently imaginary, purported to be the "Secret History of an Amour between two Persons of Condition." "The British Recluse" was in sub-title the "Secret History of Cleomira," and "Cleomelia: or, the Generous Mistress" claimed to be the "Secret History of a Lady Lately arriv'd from Bengall." The writer attached no particular significance to her use of the term, but employed it as a means of stimulating a meretricious interest in her stories. In fact she goes out of her way in the Preface to "The Injur'd Husband" to defend herself and at the same time to suggest the possibility that her novel might contain references to English contemporaries. The defence is carefully worded so that it does not constitute an absolute denial, but rather whets the curiosity.

> "It is not, therefore, to excuse my Want of Judgment in the Conduct, or my Deficiency of Expressing the Passions I have endeavour'd to represent, but to clear myself of an Accusation, which, I am inform'd, is already contrived and prepared to thunder out against me, as soon as this is publish'd, that I take this Pains. A Gentleman, who applies the little Ingenuity he is Master of to no other Study than that of sowing Dissention among those who are so unhappy, and indeed unwise, as to entertain him, either imagines, or pretends to do so, that tho' I have laid the Scene in Paris, I mean that the Adventure shou'd be thought to have happen'd in London; and that in the Character of a French Baroness I have attempted to expose the Reputation of an English Woman of Quality. I shou'd be sorry to think the Actions of any of our Ladies such as you'd give room for a

Conjecture of the Reality of what he wou'd suggest. But suppose there were indeed an Affinity between the Vices I have describ'd, and those of some Woman he knows (for doubtless if there be, she must be of his Acquaintance) I leave the World to judge to whom she is indebted for becoming the Subject of Ridicule, to me for drawing a Picture whose Original is unknown, or to him who writes her Name at the Bottom of it.

"However, if I had design'd this as a Satyr on any Person whose Crimes I had thought worthy of it, I shou'd not have thought the Resentment of such a one considerable enough to have obliged me to deny it. But as I have only related a Story, which a particular Friend of mine assures me is Matter of Fact, and happen'd at the Time when he was in Paris: I wou'd not have it made Use of as an Umbrage for the Tongue of Scandal to blast the Character of anyone, a Stranger to such detested Guilt."

Before long the term "secret history" fell into disrepute, so that writers found it necessary to make a special plea for the veracity of their work. "The Double Marriage," "The Mercenary Lover," and "Persecuted Virtue" were distinguished as "true secret histories," and in the Preface to "The Pair Hebrew: or, a True, but Secret History of Two Jewish Ladies, Who lately resided in London" Mrs. Haywood at once confessed the general truth of the charge against the type and defended the accuracy of her own production.

"There are so many Things, meerly the Effect of Invention, which have been published, of late, under the Title of SECRET HISTORIES, that, to distinguish this, I am obliged to inform my Reader, that I have not inserted one Incident which was not related to me by a Person nearly concerned in the Family of that unfortunate Gentleman, who had no other Consideration in the Choice of a Wife, than to gratify a present Passion for the Enjoyment of her Beauty."

About 1729 Eliza Haywood seems to have found the word "Life" or "Memoirs" on the title-page a more effective means for gaining the credence of her readers, and after that time she wrote, in name at least, no more secret histories. The fictions so denominated in "Secret

Histories, Novels and Poems" were in no way different from her novels, and had only the slightest, if any, foundation in fact.

A novel actually based upon a real occurrence, however, is "Dalinda, or the Double Marriage. Being the Genuine History of a very Recent, and Interesting Adventure" (1749), not certainly known to have been written by Mrs. Haywood, but bearing in the turns of expression, the letters, and the moralized ending, almost indubitable marks of her handiwork. One at least of her favorite quotations comes in at an appropriate point, and the Preface to the Reader states that the author's sole design is to show the danger of inadvertently giving way to the passions—a stock phrase with the author of "Love in Excess." The "Monthly Review" informs us that the story is "the affair betwixt Mr. Cresswell and Miss Scrope, thrown into the form of a novel."[1] The situation is somewhat similar to that described in "The Mercenary Lover."

Dalinda's unhappy passion for Malvolio incites him to ruin her, and though he deludes her with an unregistered marriage at the Fleet, he has no scruples against marrying the rich Flavilla. Wishing to possess both Flavilla's fortune and Dalinda's charms, he effects a reconciliation with the latter by promising to own their prior contract, but when he comes out into the open and proposes to entertain her as a mistress, she indignantly returns to her grandmother's house, where she summons her brother and her faithful lover, Leander, to force her perfidious husband to do her justice. The latter half of the novel is a tissue of intrigue upon intrigue, with a complication of lawsuits and letters in which Malvolio's villainy is fully exposed, and he is forced to separate from Flavilla, but is unable to exert his claims upon Dalinda. She in turn cannot wring from him any compensation, nor can she in conscience recompense the faithful love of Leander while her husband is living. Thus all parties are sufficiently unhappy to make their ways a warning to the youth of both sexes.

Evidently the history, though indeed founded on fact, differs from the works of Mrs. Haywood's imagination only in the tedious length of the legal proceedings and the uncertainty of the outcome. The only reason for basing the story on the villainy of Mr. Cresswell was to take advantage of the momentary excitement over the scandal. A similar appeal to the passion for diving into the intrigues of the great is apparent

---

1. *Monthly Review*, I, 238. July, 1749.

in the title of a novel of 1744, "The Fortunate Foundlings: Being the Genuine History of Colonel M——rs, and his Sister, Madame du P——y, the issue of the Hon. Ch——es M——rs. Son of the late Duke of R——L——D. Containing many wonderful Accidents that befel them in their Travels, and interspersed with the Characters and Adventures of Several Persons of Condition, in the most polite Courts of Europe." The Preface after the usual assurances that the work is compiled from original documents and is therefore more veracious than "the many Fictions which have been lately imposed upon the World, under the specious Titles of Secret Histories, Memoirs, &c," informs us that the purpose of the publication is to encourage virtue in both sexes by showing the amiableness of it in real characters. Instead of exposing vice in the actions of particular persons, the book is a highly moral laudation of those scions of the house of Manners whose names are adumbrated in the title. It cannot, therefore, be classed as a scandal novel or secret history.

The latter term, though loosely applied to the short tale of passion for the purpose of stimulating public curiosity, meant strictly only that type of pseudo-historical romance which interpreted actual history in the light of court intrigue. In France a flood of histories, annals, anecdotes, and memoirs,—secret, gallant, and above all true,—had been pouring from the press since 1665. The writers of these works proceeded upon the ostensible theory that secret history in recognizing woman's influence upon the destiny of nations was more true than "pure" history, which took into account only religious, political, social, or moral factors in judging the conduct of kings and statesmen. Did not Anthony suffer the world to slip from his fingers for the love of Cleopatra? Although the grand romances had a little exhausted the vein of classical material, Mme Durand-Bedacier and Mme de Villedieu compiled sundry annals of Grecian and Roman gallantry.[2] But the cycle of French secret history was much more extensive. Romancing historians ferreted out a prodigious amount of intrigue in every court from that of Childeric to Louis XIV, and set out to remodel the chronicle of the realm from the standpoint of the heart. Nearly every reign and every romantic hero was the subject of one or more "monographs," among which Mme de La Fayette's "Princesse de Clèves" takes a prominent place. The thesaurus and omnium gatherum of

---

2. Mme de Villedieu, *Annales galantes de Grece* and *Les exiles de la cour d'Auguste*. Mme Durand-Bedacier, *Les belles Grecques, ou l'histoire des plus fameuses courtisanes de la Grece.*

GEORGE WHICHER

the genus was Sauval's "Intrigues galantes de la cour de France" (1695), of which Dunlop remarks that "to a passion, which has, no doubt, especially in France, had considerable effect in state affairs, there is assigned. . . a paramount influence." But romancers with a nose for gallantry had no difficulty in finding material for their pens in England during the times of Henry VIII, Elizabeth, and Henrietta Maria. But most frequently of all was chosen the life of the Queen of Scots.

From fifteen or sixteen French biographies of the romantic Mary[3] Mrs. Haywood drew materials for an English work of two hundred and forty pages. "Mary Stuart, Queen of Scots: Being the Secret History of her Life, and the Real Causes of all Her Misfortunes. Containing a Relation of many particular Transactions in her Reign; never yet Published in any Collection" (1725) is distinguishable from her true fiction only by the larger proportion of events between set scenes of burning passion which formed the chief constituent of Eliza's romances. As history it is worthless, and its significance as fiction lies merely in its attempt to incorporate imaginative love scenes with historical fact. It was apparently compiled hastily to compete with a rival volume, "The History of the Life and Reign of Mary Stuart," published a week earlier, and it enjoyed but a languid sale. Early in 1726 it passed into a second edition, which continued to be advertised as late as 1743.

"Mary Stuart" is the only one of Mrs. Haywood's romances that strictly deserves the name of secret history. But late in 1749 a little romance that satisfied nearly all the conditions of the type insinuated itself into the pamphlet shops without the agency of any publisher. "A Letter from H——G——g, Esq. One of the Gentlemen of the Bedchamber to the Young Chevalier, and the only Person of his own Retinue that attended him from Avignon, in his late Journey through Germany, and elsewhere; Containing Many remarkable and affecting Occurrences which happened to the P—— during the course of his mysterious Progress" has been assigned to Mrs. Haywood by the late Mr. Andrew Lang,[4] perhaps on the authority of the notice in the "Monthly Review" already quoted.

The pretended author of the letter was a certain Henry Goring, a gentleman known to be in attendance upon the last of the Stuarts. The preface gives a commonplace explanation of how the letter fell into

---

3. B.M. Catalogue.
4. A. Lang, *History of English Literature* (1912), 458. See *ante*, p. 25.

the hands of the editor through a similarity of names. Apparently the pamphlet was thought seditious because it eulogized the Young Chevalier, hinting how advantageous it would be to have him on the throne. As the secret journey progresses, the Prince has a chance to expose his admirable political tenets in conversation with a nobleman of exalted rank; in rescuing a young woman from a fire, caring for her in distress, and refusing to take advantage of her passion for him, he gives evidence of a morality not accorded him by history and proves "how fit he is to govern others, who knows so well how to govern himself"; and when assaulted by hired assassins, he manifests courage and coolness, killing one of the bravos with his own hand. It is unnecessary to review the various stages in the Pretender's travels, which are related with a great air of mystery, but amount to nothing. The upshot is that the Prince has not renounced all thoughts of filling the throne of his ancestors, but has ends in view which the world knows nothing of and which will surprise them all some day. Had the Prince shown himself more susceptible to the charms of the merchants' daughters who fell in his way, this bit of romancing might claim the doubtful distinction of being Mrs. Haywood's only original secret history, but as it stands, no part of the story has the necessary motivation by passion. The intrigue is entirely political.

There would seem to be little dangerous stuff in this performance even five years after the insurrection of 1745, but if as the "Monthly Review" ill-naturedly hints, Eliza Haywood really suffered for her supposed connection with it, the lesson was at any rate effectual, for the small references to the P—— occasionally noticeable in her previous works suddenly ceased, and thereafter the novelist scrupulously refrained from mingling fiction and politics. Previously, however, she had at least once attempted to write a political satire elaborately disguised as a romance. In July, 1736, according to the list of books in the "Gentleman's Magazine," numerous duodecimo volumes emanated from the shop of S. Baker and were sold under the title of "Adventures of Eovaai, Princess of Ijaveo. A Pre-Adamitical History. Interspersed with a great Number of remarkable Occurrences, which happened, and may again happen, to several Empires, Kingdoms, Republicks, and particular Great Men. . . Written originally in the Language of Nature, (of later Years but little understood.) First translated into Chinese. . . and now retranslated into English, by the Son of a Mandarin, residing in London."[5]

---

5. Re-issued as *The Unfortunate Princess, or, the Ambitious Statesman*, 1741.

After the introduction has given a fantastic account of the Pre-Adamitical world, and explained with elaborate unconvincingness how the manuscript of the book came into existence, the tale commences like a moral allegory, but soon lapses into mere extravagant adventure. Capable at all times of using a *deus ex machina* as the readiest way of solving a situation, Mrs. Haywood here makes immoderate use of magic elements.

Eojaeu, King of Ijaveo, leaves to his daughter, Eovaai, a precious jewel, upon the keeping of which her happiness depends. One day as she is gazing at it in the garden, it slips from its setting and is carried away by a little bird. Immediately the princess is forsaken by her quarreling subjects and abandoned by her suitors, save only the wicked Ochihatou, prime minister of the neighboring kingdom of Hypotofa, who has gained ascendancy over his sovereign by black magic, caused the promising young prince to be banished, and used his power to promote his ambitions and lusts. By infernal agencies he conveys Eovaai to the Hypotofan court, where he corrupts her mind and is about to triumph in her charms when he is summoned to quell a political disturbance. The princess, left languishing in a bower, is saved by her good Genius, who enables her to discern the true deformity of her betrayer and to escape to the castle of the good Alhahuza, and ultimately into the kingdom of Oozoff, where Ochihatou's magic has no power over her. During her stay there she listens to much political theorizing of a republican trend. Ochihatou succeeds in kidnapping her, and she is only saved from his loathed embraces by discovering one of his former mistresses in the form of a monkey whom she manages to change back into human shape and substitutes in her stead. While the statesman is employed as a lover, the populace led by Alhahuza storm the palace. Ochihatou discovers the trick that has been played upon him, hastily transforms his unlucky mistress into a rat, and conveys himself and Eovaai through the air into a kingdom near at hand, where he hopes to make head against the rebels. His pretensions are encouraged, but learning by his magic that the Hypotofan monarch has been freed from the power of his spells, he persuades the princess to return to Ijaveo with him in hopes of regaining her kingdom. He transforms her into a dove, himself into a vulture, and flies with her to a wood near the Ijavean court. There he restores their natural shapes and makes a base attack upon her honor. In the struggle she manages to break his wand, and he in a fury hangs her up by the hair and is about to scourge her to death, when she is rescued by a glorious young stranger. The wicked Ochihatou dashes his brains out against an oak. Her deliverer turns out to be the banished prince of Hypotofa, who restores to her the lost jewel, weds her, and prosperously governs their united realms.

The fantastic story, however, was probably little calculated to sell the book. It was addressed to those who could read between the lines well enough to discern particular personages in the characters of the fiction, and especially a certain great man in the figure of the evil prime minister.

In 1736 when Eliza's novel first appeared, Walpole's defeated Excise Bill of 1733–4 and his policy of non-interference on the Continent had made him cordially disliked by the people, and by 1741 his unpopular ministry, like Lady Mary Montagu's stairs, was "in a declining way." Sir Robert had never shown himself a friend to letters, and there were not a few writers, among them one so illustrious as Henry Fielding, who were ready to seize upon any pretext for attacking him.[6] There can be no doubt that in the character of the villainous, corrupt, greedy, vain, lascivious, but plausible Ochihatou Mrs. Haywood intended her readers to recognize a semblance of the English minister. "Of all the statesmen who have held high office, it would be impossible to find one who has been more systematically abused and more unjustly treated than Sir Robert Walpole. . . He is the 'Father of Parliamentary Corruption,' the 'foe to English liberty,' the 'man who maintained his power by the basest and most venal tactics' . . . Whenever his administration is alluded to in Parliament a shudder runs through the House. . . at the very thought that one so sordid, so interested, so schemingly selfish, should have attained to the position of Prime Minister, and have commanded a following. If we read the pamphlet literature of the eighteenth century, we see Walpole represented as the meanest and most corrupt of mankind."[7] Lord Chesterfield says of him: "His prevailing weakness was to be thought to have a polite and happy turn to gallantry, of which he had undoubtedly less than any man living; it

6. J.E. Wells, *Fielding's Political Purpose in Jonathan Wilde*, PMLA, XXVIII, No. I, pp. 1–55. March, 1913. See also *The Secret History of Mama Oello*, 1733. "The Curaca Robilda's Character (i.e. Sir Robert Walpole's) will inform you that there were Evil Ministers even amongst the simple Indians" . . . and *The Statesman's Progress: Or, Memoirs of the Life, Administration, and Fall of Houly Chan, Primier Minister to Abensader, Emperor of China* (1733).
7. A.C. Ewald, *Sir Robert Walpole* (1878), 444.

was his favorite and frequent subject of conversation, which proved, to those who had any penetration, that it was his prevailing weakness, and they applied to it with success."[8] And Lord Hervey reports that the Queen remarked of Walpole's mistress, "dear Molly Skerritt": "She must be a clever gentlewoman to have made him believe she cares for him on any other score (but his money); and to show you what fools we all are in some point or other, she has certainly told him some fine story or other of her love and her passion, and that poor man—*avec ce gros corps, ces jambes enflées, et ce vilain ventre*—believes her. Ah! what is human nature!"[9]

With this sketch of Walpole compare the account of Ochihatou, Prime Minister of Hypotofa. "This great Man was born of a mean Extraction, and so deformed in his own Person, that not even his own Parents cou'd look on him with Satisfaction. . . As he was extremely amorous, and had so little in him to inspire the tender Passion, the first Proof he gave of his Art, was to. . . cast such a Delusion before the Eyes of all who saw him, that he appeared to them such as he wished to be, a most comely and graceful Man.

"With this Advantage, join'd to the most soothing and insinuating Behaviour, he came to Court, and, by his Artifices, so wound himself into the Favour of some great Officers, that he was not long without being put into a considerable Post. This he discharged so well, that he was soon promoted to a better, and at length to those of the highest Trust and Honour in the Kingdom. But that which was most remarkable in him, and very much contributed to endear him to all Sorts of People, was that his Elevation did not seem to have made the least Change in his Sentiments. His natural Pride, his Lust, his exorbitant Ambition, were disguised under the Appearance of Sweetness of Disposition, Chastity, and even more Condescension, than was consistent with the Rank he then possest. By this Behaviour, he render'd himself so far from exciting Envy, that those, by whose Recommendation he had obtained what he enjoy'd, and with some of whom he was now on more than an Equality, wish'd rather to see an Augmentation, than Diminution of a Power he so well knew to use; and so successful was his Hypocrisy, that the most Discerning saw not into his Designs, till he found means to accomplish

---

8. A.C. Ewald, *Sir Robert Walpole*, 450.
9. Lord Hervey's *Memoirs*, London, 1884, II, 143.

them, to the almost total Ruin of both King and People."[10] Ochihatou worms his way into the favor of the king, and after gaining complete ascendancy over his royal master, uses the power for his own ends. He fills the positions at court with wretches subservient to his own interests. "He next proceeded to seize the publick Treasure into his own Hands, which he converted not to Works of Justice or Charity, or any Uses for the Honour of the Kingdom, but in building stately Palaces for himself, his Wives, and Concubines, and enriching his mean Family, and others who adhered to him, and assisted in his Enterprizes." Lest this reference should not be plain enough in its application to Walpole's extravagances at Houghton, Mrs. Haywood adds in a footnote, "Our Author might have saved himself the Trouble of particularizing in what manner Ochihatou apply'd the Nation's Money; since he had said enough in saying, he was a *Prime Minister*, to make the Reader acquainted with his Conduct in that Point." Further allusions to a standing army of mercenaries and to an odious tribe of tax-collectors—two of the most popular grievances against Walpole—give additional force to the satire. There is a suspicion that in the character of the young prince banished by Ochihatou readers of a right turn of mind were intended to perceive a cautious allusion to the Pretender.

That Walpole not only perceived, but actively resented the affront, we may infer, though evidence is lacking, from the six years of silence that followed the publication of the satire. Perhaps the government saw fit to buy off the troublesome author by a small appointment, but such indulgent measures were not usually applied to similar cases. More probably Eliza found it wise to seek in France or some neighboring country the safety from the malignant power of the Prime Minister that her heroine sought in the kingdom of Oozoff.

The "Adventures of Eovaai" contains almost the last of the dedications written in a servile tone to a patron whose favor Mrs. Haywood hoped to curry. Henceforward she was to be more truly a woman of letters in that her books appealed ostensibly at least only to the reading public. The victim of her final eulogy was the redoubtable Sarah, Duchess Dowager of Marlborough, who, when finding herself addressed as "O most illustrious Wife, and Parent of the Greatest, Best, and Loveliest! it was not sufficient for you to adorn Posterity with the Amiableness of every Virtue," etc., etc., may perhaps have recalled how her shining

---

10. *The Unfortunate Princess*, 18, etc.

character had been blackened some twelve years before in a licentious volume called "Memoirs of a Certain Island adjacent to the Kingdom of Utopia."[11] Had her Grace been aware that the reputed author of that comprehensive lampoon was none other than the woman who now outdid herself in praise, Eliza Haywood would probably have profited little by her panegyric. For though the "Memoirs of a Certain Island" like the "Adventures of Eovaai" made a pretence of being translated into English from the work of a celebrated Utopian author, the British public found no difficulty in attributing it by popular acclaim to Mrs. Haywood, and she reaped immense notoriety from it. In prefaces to some of her subsequent works she complained of the readiness of the world to pick meanings in whatever was published by a struggling woman, or protested that she had no persons or families in view in writing her stories, but she never disclaimed the authorship of this production. Undoubtedly the world was right in "smoking" the writer.[12]

If before she had retailed secret histories of late amours singly, Mrs. Haywood dealt in them now by the wholesale, and any reader curious to know the identity of the personages hidden under such fictitious names as Romanus, Beaujune, Orainos, Davilla, Flirtillaria, or Saloida could obtain the information by consulting a convenient "key" affixed to each of the two volumes. In this respect, as in the general scheme of her work, Mrs. Haywood was following the model set by the celebrated Mrs. Manley in her "New Atalantis." She in turn had derived her method from the French *romans à clef* or romances in which contemporary scandal was reported in a fictitious disguise. The imitation written by Mrs. Haywood became only less notorious than her original, and was still well enough known in 1760 to be included in the convenient list of novels prefixed to the elder Colman's "Polly Honeycombe." It consists of a tissue of anecdotes which, if retold, would (in Fuller's words) "stain through the cleanest language I can wrap them in," all set in an allegorical framework of a commonplace kind.

---

11. *Memoirs of a Certain Island*, II, 249. "Marama (the Duchess of Marlborough) has been for many Years a Grandmother; but Age is the smallest of her Imperfections:—She is of a Disposition so perverse and peevish, so designing, mercenary, proud, cruel, and revengeful, that it has been a matter of debate, if she were really Woman, or if some Fiend had not assumed that Shape on purpose to affront the Sex, and fright Mankind from Marriage."

12. J. Nichols, *Literary Anecdotes*, III, 649, records the tradition that Chapman was the publisher of Mrs. Haywood's *Utopia*.

A noble youth arrives upon the shores of a happy island (England), where he encounters the God of Love, who conveys him to a spacious court in the midst of the city. There Pecunia and Fortuna, served by their high priest Lucitario (J. Craggs, the elder) preside over an Enchanted Well (South Sea Company) while all degrees of humanity stand about in expectation of some wonderful event. From amid the throng the God of Love selects certain persons as examples of perverted love. The stories he relates about them range from mere anecdotes to elaborate histories containing several love-letters. In substance these tales consist of the grossest scandal that could be collected from the gossip of profligate society. After hearing more than a satiety of these illustrations, the youth beholds the Genius of the Isle, supported by Astrea and Reason, exposing the fraud of the Enchanted Well to the dismay of the greedy rabble. The young stranger then sinks to rest in a perfumed bower, while the God of Love and the Genius of the Isle set about a much needed reformation of manners.

None of the skimmings of contemporary gossip poured out in the two volumes deserves the least consideration, save such as reveal the fair writer's relations with other authors. In return for Savage's eulogy of her "Love in Excess" and "Rash Resolve" the scribbling dame included in her scandal novel the story of his noble parentage substantially as it had already been told by Aaron Hill in the "Plain Dealer" for 24 June, 1724. But in addition she prefaced the account with a highly colored narrative of the amours of Masonia and Riverius.[13] However much the author of "The Bastard" may have desired to prove his noble origin, he might easily have resented a too open flaunting of his mother's disgrace. Moreover, Mrs. Haywood hinted that his unfeeling mother was not the only woman whom the poet had to fear. By the insinuations of a female fury, a pretender to the art of poetry, for whom Eliza has no words too black—in fact some of her epithets are too shady to be quoted—he has been led into actions, mean, unjust, and wicked. The vile woman, it seems, has been guilty of defaming the reputations of others.

"The Monster whose Soul is wholly compos'd of Hipocrisy, Envy, and Lust, can ill endure another Woman should be esteem'd Mistress of those Virtues she has acted with too barefaced an Impudence to

---

13. Anne Mason, formerly Lady Macclesfield, and the Earl of Rivers, whom Savage claimed as his father.

GEORGE WHICHER

pretend to, and is never so happy as when by some horrid Stratagem she finds the means to traduce and blast the Character of the Worthy. . . With how much readiness the easily deceiv'd Riverius (Savage) has obliged her in spreading those Reports, coin'd in the hellish Mint of her own Brain, I am sorry to say. . . It cannot be doubted but that he has lost many Friends on her account, in particular one there was who bore him a singular Respect, tho' no otherways capacitated to serve him than by good Wishes.—This Person receiv'd a more than common Injury from him, thro' the Instigations of that female Fury; but yet continuing to acknowledge his good Qualities, and pitying his falling into the contrary, took no other Revenge than writing a little Satire, which his having publish'd some admirable fine things in the praise of Friendship and Honour, gave a handsome opportunity for." (Vol. I, p. 184.)

From the exceptional animus displayed by Eliza Haywood in describing her colleague in the school for scandal, one may suspect that the lightning had struck fairly near home. One is almost forced to believe that Savage's well-wisher, the writer of the little satire, "To the Ingenious Riverius, on his writing in the Praise of Friendship," was none other than Eliza herself.[14] Exactly what injury she had sustained from him and his Siren is not known, but although he still stood high in her esteem, she was implacable against that "worse than Lais" whom in a long and pungent description she satirized under the name of Gloatitia.

"Behold another. . . in everything as ridiculous, in some more vile—that big-bone'd, buxom, brown Woman. . . Of all the Gods there is none she acknowledges but Phoebus, him she frequently implores for assistance, to charm her Lovers with the Spirit of Poetry. . . She pretends, however, to have an intimate acquaintance with the Muses—has judgment enough to know that *ease* and *please* make a Rhyme, and to count ten Syllables on her Fingers.—This is the Stock with which she sets up for a Wit, and among some ignorant Wretches passes for such; but with People of true Understanding, nothing affords

14. She had a way of rechristening her friends by romantic titles. See her poem, "To Mr. Walter Bowman. . . Occasion'd by his objecting against my giving the Name of Hillarius to Aaron Hill, Esq."

more subject of ridicule, than that incoherent Stuff which she calls Verses.—She bribed, with all the Favours she is capable of conferring, a Bookseller (Curll) (famous for publishing soft things) to print some of her Works, ("The Amours of Clio and Strephon," 1719) on which she is not a little vain: tho' she might very well have spared herself the trouble. Few Men, of any rank whatsoever, but have been honour'd with the receipt of some of her Letters both in Prose and Measure—few Coffee-Houses but have been the Repository of them."[15]

The student of contemporary secret history does not need to refer to the "key" to discover that the woman whose power to charm Savage was so destructive to Eliza's peace of mind was that universal mistress of minor poets, the Mira of Thomson, the Clio of Dyer and Hill, the famous Martha Fowke, who at the time happened to have fixed the scandal of her affections upon the Volunteer Laureate.[16] That the poet's opinion of her remained unchanged by Mrs. Haywood's vituperation may be inferred from some lines in her praise in a satire called "The Authors of the Town," printed soon after the publication of "Memoirs of a Certain Island."[17]

> "Clio, descending Angels sweep thy Lyre,
> Prompt thy soft Lays, and breathe Seraphic Fire.
> Tears fall, Sighs rise, obedient to thy Strains,
> And the Blood dances in the mazy Veins! . . .
> In social Spirits, lead thy Hours along,
> Thou Life of Loveliness, thou Soul of Song!"

But not content with singing the praises of her rival, Savage cast a slur upon Mrs. Haywood's works and even upon the unfortunate dame herself.

---

15. *Memoirs of a Certain Island*, I, 43–7 condensed.

16. For an account of Clio see an article by Bolton Corney, "James Thomson and David Mallet," *Athenaeum*, II, 78, 1859. And Miss Dorothy Brewster, *Aaron Hill*, 188. Her unsavory biography entitled *Clio, or a Secret History of the Amours of Mrs. S-n—m*, was still known at the time of *Polly Honeycombe*, 1760.

17. *The Authors of the Town; a Satire. Inscribed to the Author of the Universal Passion*. For J. Roberts, 1725. A number of lines from this poem appear later in Savage's "On False Historians," *Poems* (Cooke's ed.), II, 189.

> *"First, let me view what noxious Nonsense reigns,*
> *While yet I loiter on Prosaic Plains;*
> *If Pens impartial active Annals trace,*
> *Others, with secret Histr'y, Truth deface:*
> *Views and Reviews, and wild Memoirs appear,*
> *And Slander darkens each recorded year."*

After relating at some length the typical absurdities of the *chronique scandaleuse*—deaths by poison, the inevitably dropped letter, and intrigues of passion and jealousy—he became more specific in describing various authors. Among others

> *"A cast-off Dame, who of Intrigues can judge,*
> *Writes Scandal in Romance—A Printer's Drudge!*
> *Flush'd with Success, for Stage-Renown she pants,*
> *And melts, and swells, and pens luxurious Rants."*

The first two lines might apply to the notorious Mrs. Manley, lately deceased, who had for sometime been living as a hack writer for Alderman Barber, but she had written no plays since "Lucius" in 1717. Mrs. Haywood, however, equally a cast-off dame and a printer's drudge, had recently produced her "Fair Captive," a most luxurious rant. The passage, then, may probably refer to her.

If, as is possible, the poem was circulated in manuscript before its publication, this intended insult may be the injury complained of by Mrs. Haywood in "Memoirs of a Certain Island." Though she was content to retaliate only by heaping coals of fire upon the poet's bays, and though she even heightens the pathos of his story by relating how he had refused the moiety of a small pension from his mother upon hearing that she had suffered losses in the collapse of the South Sea scheme, Savage remained henceforth her implacable enemy. Perhaps her abuse of the divine Clio, the suspected instigator of his attacks upon her, may have been an unforgivable offense.

No need to particularize further. We need not vex the shade of Addison by repeating what Eliza records of his wild kinsman, Eustace Budgell (Bellario). No other person of literary note save Aaron Hill, favorably mentioned as Lauranus, appears in all the dreary two volumes. The vogue of the book was not due to its merits as fiction, which are slight, but to the spiciness of personal allusions. That such reading was appreciated even in the highest circles is shown by young Lady Mary Pierrepont's defence of Mrs. Manley's "New Atalantis."[18] In the history of the novel, however, the *roman à clef* deserves perhaps more recognition than has hitherto been accorded it. Specific delineation was necessary to make effective the satire, and though the presence of the "key" made broad caricature possible, since each picture was labeled, yet the writers of scandal novels usually drew their portraits with an amount of detail foreign to the method of the romancers.[19] While the tale of passion developed the novelist's power to make the emotions seem convincing, the *chronique scandaleuse* emphasized the necessity of accurate observation of real men and women. But satire and libel, though necessitating detailed description, did not, like burlesque or parody, lead to the creation of character. In that respect the "Memoirs of a Certain Island" and all its tribe are notably deficient.

A less comprehensive survey of current tittle-tattle, perhaps modeled on Mrs. Manley's "Court Intrigues" (1711), stole forth anonymously on 16 October, 1724, under the caption, "Bath-Intrigues: in four Letters to a Friend in London," a title which sufficiently indicates the nature of the work. Like the "Memoirs of a Certain Island" these letters consist of mere jottings of scandal. Most probably both productions were from the same pen, though "Bath-Intrigues" has been attributed to Mrs. Manley.[20] Opposite the title-page Roberts, the publisher, advertised "The Masqueraders," "The Fatal Secret," and "The Surprise" as by the same author. One of Mrs. Haywood's favorite quotations, used by her later as a motto for the third volume of "The Female Spectator," stands with naïve appropriateness on the title-page:

---

18. *Letters from the Lady Mary Wortley Montagu*, Everyman edition, 4.
19. Compare the picture of Gloatitia, for instance, with the following of a lady in *La Belle Assemblée*, I, 22. "To form any Idea of what she was, one must imagine all that can be conceived of Perfection—the most blooming Youth, the most delicate Complection, Eyes that had in them all the Fire of Wit, and Tenderness of Love, a Shape easy, and fine proportion'd Limbs; and to all this, a thousand unutterable Graces accompanying every Air and little Motion."
20. Miss C.E. Morgan, *The Novel of Manners*, 221. *Bath-Intrigues* was included in Mrs. Haywood's Works, 1727. Another work contained in the same two volumes, *The Perplex'd Duchess; or, Treachery Rewarded: Being some Memoirs of the Court of Malfy. In a Letter from a Sicilian Nobleman, who had his Residence there, to his Friend in London* (1728), may be a scandal novel, though the title suggests a reworking of Webster's *Duchess of Malfi*. I have not seen the book.

> *"There is a Lust in Man, no Awe can tame,*
> *Of loudly publishing his Neighbor's Shame."*

The writer of "Bath-Intrigues," moreover, did not hesitate to recommend Eliza's earlier novels to the good graces of scandal-loving readers, for she describes a certain letter as "amorous as Mrs. O——F——d's Eyes, or the Writings of the Author of Love in Excess." Most curious of all is the fact that the composer of the four letters, who signs herself J.B., refers *en passant* to Belinda's inconstancy to Sir Thomas Worthly, an allusion to the story of the second part of "The British Recluse." This reference would indicate either that there was some basis of actuality in the earlier fiction, or that Mrs. Haywood was using imaginary scandal to pad her collection. However that may be, this second *chronique scandaleuse* was apparently no less successful, though less renowned, than the first, for a third edition was imprinted during the following March.

The scribbling dame again used the feigned letter as a vehicle for mildly infamous gossip in "Letters from the Palace of Fame. Written by a First Minister in the Regions of Air, to an Inhabitant of this World. Translated from an Arabian Manuscript."[21] Its pretended source and the sham Oriental disguise make the work an unworthy member of that group of feigned Oriental letters begun by G.P. Marana with "L'Espion turc" in 1684, continued by Dufresny and his imitator, T. Brown, raised to a philosophic level by Addison and Steele, and finally culminant in Montesquieu's "Lettres Persanes" (1721) and Goldsmith's "Citizen of the World" (1760).[22] The fourth letter is a well-told Eastern adventure, dealing with the revenge of Forzio who seduces the wife of his enemy, Ben-hamar, through the agency of a Christian slave, but in general the "Letters" are valuable only as they add an atom of evidence to the popularity of pseudo-Oriental material. Eliza Haywood was anxious to give the public what it wanted. She had found a ready market for scandal, and knew that the piquancy of slander was enhanced and the writer protected from disagreeable consequences if her stories were cast in some sort of a disguise. She had already used the obvious ruse of an allegory in the "Memoirs of a Certain Island" and had just completed a

---

21. Ascribed to Mrs. Haywood in the advertisements of her additional *Works*, 1727. The B.M. copy, catalogued under "Ariel," contains only a fragment of 24 pages.
22. Miss M.P. Conant, *The Oriental Tale in England in the Eighteenth Century (1908)*, *passim*.

feigned history in the "Court of Carimania." The well known "Turkish Spy" and its imitations, or perhaps the recent but untranslated "Lettres Persanes," may have suggested to her the possibility of combining bits of gossip in letters purporting to be translated from the Arabic and written by some supermundane being. The latter part of the device had already been used by Defoe in "The Consolidator." Mrs. Haywood merely added the suggestion of a mysterious Oriental source. She makes no attempt to satirize contemporary society, but is content to retail vague bits of town talk to customers who might be deluded into imagining them of importance. "The new created Vizier," the airy correspondent reports, "might have succeeded better in another Post, than in this, which with so much earnestness he has sollicited. For, notwithstanding the Plaudits he has received from our Princess, and the natural Propensity to State-Affairs, given him by his Saturnine Genius; his Significator Mars promis'd him greater Honours in the Field, than he can possibly attain to in the Cabinet." And so on. Both "Bath-Intrigues" and "Letters from the Palace of Fame" may be classed as *romans à clef* although no "key" for either has yet been found. In all other respects they conform to type.

The only one of Mrs. Haywood's scandal novels that rivaled the fame of her "Memoirs of a Certain Island" was the notorious "Secret History of the Present Intrigues of the Court of Carimania" (1727), a feigned history on a more coherent plan than the allegorical hodge-podge of the former compilation. The incidents in this book are all loosely connected with the amours of Theodore, Prince of Carimania, with various beauties of this court. The chronicle minutely records the means he employed to overcome their scruples, to stifle their jealousies and their reproaches, and finally to extricate himself from affairs of gallantry grown tedious. Nearly all the changes are rung on the theme of amorous adventure in describing the progress of the royal rake and his associates. The "key"[23] at the end identifies the characters with various noble personages at the court of George II when Prince of Wales. The melting Lutetia, for instance, represented "Mrs. Baladin" or more accurately Mary Bellenden, maid of honor to the Princess, to whose charms Prince George was in fact not insensible. Barsina and

23. The "key" is almost the sole contribution to Mrs. Haywood's bibliography in Bohn's Lowndes. Most of the personages mentioned are described in the notes of John Wilson Croker's *Letters to and from the Countess of Suffolk* (1824).

Arilla were also maids of honor: the former became the second wife of John, Duke of Argyle (Aridanor), while the latter was that sister of Sir Sidney Meadows celebrated by Pope for her prudence. Although the "key" discreetly refrained from identifying the amorous Theodore, no great penetration was necessary to see in his character a picture of the royal George himself. A tradition not well authenticated but extremely probable states that printer and publisher were taken up in consequence of this daring scandal.

But more important in its effect upon the author's fortunes than any action of the outraged government was the resentment which her defamation of certain illustrious persons awakened in the breast of the dictator of letters. In chosing to expose in the character of her chief heroine, Ismonda, the foibles of Mrs. Henrietta Howard, the neighbor of Pope, the friend of Swift and Arbuthnot, and the admired of Lord Peterborough, Mrs. Haywood made herself offensive in the nostrils of the literary trio. The King's mistress, later the Countess of Suffolk, conducted herself with such propriety that her friends affected to believe that her relations with her royal lover were purely platonic, and they naturally failed to welcome the chronicle of her amours and the revelation of the slights which George II delighted to inflict upon her. Swift described the writer of the scandal as a "stupid, infamous, scribbling woman";[24] Peterborough writing to Lady Mary Montagu in behalf of his friend, the English Homer, sneered at the "four remarkable poetesses and scribblers, Mrs. Centlivre, Mrs. Haywood, Mrs. Manley, and Mrs. Ben (*sic*)";[25] and Pope himself pilloried the offender to all time in his greatest satire.

---

24. The Correspondence of Jonathan Swift, ed. by F. Elrington Ball (1913), Vol. IV, 264, 266. The Countess of Suffolk, in a playful attack on Swift, wrote (25 Sept. 1731) . . . "I should not have despaired, that. . . this Irish patriot. . . should have closed the scene under suspicions of having a violent passion for Mrs. Barber, and Lady M—— (Montagu) or Mrs. Haywood have writ the progress of it." In reply Swift wrote (26 Oct. 1731) that he could not guess who was intended by Lady M—— and that he had heard Mrs. Haywood characterized in the terms quoted above.
25. Elwin and Courthope's *Pope*, III, 279.

V

The Heroine of "The Dunciad"

M r. Pope's devious efforts to make the gratification of his personal animosities seem due to public-spirited indignation have been generally exposed. Beside the overwhelming desire to spite Theobald for his presumption in publishing "Shakespeare Restored" the aggrieved poet was actuated by numerous petty grudges against the inhabitants of Grub Street, all of which he masked behind a pretence of righteous zeal. According to the official explanation "The Dunciad" was composed with the most laudable motive of damaging those writers of "abusive falsehoods and scurrilities" who "had aspersed almost all the great characters of the age; and this with impunity, their own persons and names being utterly secret and obscure." He intended to seize the "opportunity of doing some good, by detecting and dragging into light these common enemies of mankind; since to invalidate this universal slander, it sufficed to show what contemptible men were the authors of it. He was not without hopes, that by manifesting the dulness of those who had only malice to recommend them, either the booksellers would not find their account in employing them, or the men themselves, when discovered, would want courage to proceed in so unlawful an occupation. This it was that gave birth to the 'Dunciad,' and he thought it a happiness, that by the late flood of slander on himself, he had acquired such a peculiar right over their names as was necessary to this design."[1] But gentlemanly reproof and delicate satire would be wasted on "libellers and common nuisances." They must be met upon their own ground and overwhelmed with filth. "Thus the politest men are obliged sometimes to swear when they have to do with porters and oyster-wenches." Moreover, those unexceptionable models, Homer, Virgil, and Dryden had all admitted certain nasty expressions, and in comparison with them "our author. . . tosses about his dung with an air of majesty."[2] In the episode devoted to the "authoress of those most scandalous books called the Court of Carimania, and the new Utopia,"

1. Elwin and Courthope's *Pope*, IV, 4.
2. Elwin and Courthope's *Pope*, IV, 135, note 3.

GEORGE WHICHER

remarks the annotator of "The Dunciad, Variorum," "is exposed, in the most contemptuous manner, the profligate licentiousness of those shameless scribblers (for the most part of that sex, which ought least to be capable of such malice or impudence) who in libellous Memoirs and Novels, reveal the faults and misfortunes of both sexes, to the ruin of public fame, or disturbance of private happiness. Our good poet (by the whole cast of his work being obliged not to take off the irony) where he could not show his indignation, hath shewn his contempt, as much as possible; having here drawn as vile a picture as could be represented in the colours of Epic poesy."[3] On these grounds Pope justified the coarseness of his allusions to Mrs. Thomas (Corinna) and Eliza Haywood. But a statement of high moral purpose from the author of "The Dunciad" was almost inevitably the stalking-horse of an unworthy action. Mr. Pope's reasons, real and professed, for giving Mrs. Haywood a particularly obnoxious place in his epic of dullness afford a curious illustration of his unmatched capacity ostensibly to chastise the vices of the age, while in fact hitting an opponent below the belt.

The scourge of dunces had, as we have seen, a legitimate cause to resent the licentious attack upon certain court ladies, especially his friend Mrs. Howard, in a scandalous fiction of which Eliza Haywood was the reputed author. Besides she had allied herself with Bond, Defoe, and other inelegant pretenders in the domain of letters, and was known to be the friend of Aaron Hill, Esq., who stood not high in Pope Alexander's good graces. And finally Pope may have honestly believed that she was responsible for a lampoon upon him in person. In "A List of Books, Papers, and Verses, in which our Author was Abused, Before the Publication of the Dunciad; with the True Names of the Authors," appended to "The Dunciad, Variorum" of 1729, Mrs. Haywood was credited with an anonymous "Memoirs of Lilliput, octavo, printed in 1727."[4] The full title of the work in question reads, "Memoirs of the Court of Lilliput. Written by Captain Gulliver. Containing an Account of the Intrigues, and someother particular Transactions of that Nation, omitted in the two Volumes of his Travels. Published by Lucas Bennet, with a Preface, shewing how these Papers fell into his hands." The title, indeed, is suggestive of such productions as "The

---

3. Elwin and Courthope's *Pope*, IV, 141.
4. Elwin and Courthope's *Pope*, IV, 232. Professor Lounsbury has apparently confused this work with *A Cursory View of the History of Lilliput For these last forty three Years*, 8vo, 1727, a political satire containing no allusion to Pope. See *The Text of Shakespeare*, 287.

Court of Carimania." In the Preface Mr. Lucas Bennet describes himself as a schoolfellow and friend of Captain Gulliver, which is reason enough to make us doubt his own actuality. But whether a real personage or a pseudonym for someother author, he was probably not Mrs. Haywood, for the style of the book is unlike that of her known works, and the historian of Lilliput indulges in some mild sarcasms at the expense of women who "set up for Writers, before they have well learned their Alphabet," Either before or after composing his lines on Eliza, however, Pope chose to attribute the volume to her. The passage which doubtless provoked his noble rage against shameless scribblers was part of a debate between Lilliputian Court ladies who were anxious lest their having been seen by Gulliver in a delicate situation should reflect on their reputations. The speaker undertakes to reassure her companions.

> "And besides, the inequality of our Stature rightly consider'd, ought to be for us as full a Security from Slander, as that between Mr. P—pe, and those *great* Ladies who do nothing without him; admit him to their Closets, their Bed-sides, consult him in the choice of their Servents, their Garments, and make no scruple of putting them on or off before him: Everybody knows they are Women of strict Virtue, and he a Harmless Creature, who has neither the Will, nor Power of doing any farther Mischief than with his Pen, and that he seldom draws, but in defense of their Beauty; or to second their Revenge against some presuming Prude, who boasts a Superiority of Charms: or in privately transcribing and passing for his own, the elaborate Studies of some more learned Genius."[5]

Such an attack upon the sensitive poet's person and pride did not go unnoticed. More than a year later he returned the slur with interest upon the head of the supposed author. The lines on Eliza, which still remain the coarsest in the satire, were in the original "Dunciad" even more brutal.[6] Nothing short of childish personal animus could account for the filthy malignity of Pope's revenge.

---

5. *Memoirs of the Court of Lilliput*, 16.
6. *The Dunciad*. 1728. Book II, lines 137–48, and 170; Book III, lines 149–53.

GEORGE WHICHER

> *"See in the circle next, Eliza plac'd;*
> *Two babes of love close clinging to her waste;*
> *Fair as before her works she stands confess'd*
> *In flow'r'd brocade by bounteous* Kirkall *dress'd,*
> *Pearls on her neck, and roses in her hair,*
> *And her fore-buttocks to the navel bare."*[7]

The Goddess of Dullness offers "yon Juno of majestic size" as the chief prize in the booksellers' games. "Chetwood and Curll accept this glorious strife," the latter, as always, wins the obscene contest, "and the pleas'd dame soft-smiling leads away." Nearly all of this account is impudent slander, but Mr. Pope's imputations may have had enough truth in them to sting. His description of Eliza is a savage caricature of her portrait by Kirkall prefixed to the first edition of her collected novels, plays, and poems (1724).[8] Curll's "Key to the Dunciad," quoted with evident relish by Pope in the Variorum notes, recorded on the authority of contemporary scandal that the "two babes of love" were the offspring of a poet[9] and a bookseller. This bit of libel meant no more than that Mrs. Haywood's relations with Savage and other minor writers had been injudiciously unconventional. As for the booksellers, Curll had not been professionally connected with the authoress before the publication of "The Dunciad," and the part he played in the games may be regarded as due entirely to Pope's malice. W. R. Chetwood was indeed the first publisher of Eliza's effusions, but his name was even more strongly associated with the prize which actually fell to his lot.[10] In 1735 Chapman was substituted for Chetwood, and in the last revision Thomas Osborne, then the object of Pope's private antipathy, gained a permanent place as Curll's opponent. Taken all in all, the chief virulence of the abuse was directed more against the booksellers than against Mrs. Haywood.

The second mention of Eliza was also in connection with Corinna in a passage now canceled.

---

7. Elwin and Courthope's *Pope*, IV, 282.

8. A second engraving by Vertue after Parmentier formed the frontispiece of *Secret Histories, Novels, and Poems*.

9. E. Curll, *Key to the Dunciad*, 12. Some copies apparently read "peer" for "poet." See Elwin and Courthope's *Pope*, IV, 330, note pp.; and Sir Sidney Lee, article *Haywood* in the D.N.B.

10. Elwin and Courthope's *Pope*, IV, 330, note ss.

> *"See next two slip-shod* Muses *traipse along,*
> *In lofty madness meditating song,*
> *With tresses staring from poetic dreams*
> *And never wash'd, but in* Castalia's *streams.*
> *H—— and T——, glories of their race!"*[11]

The first initial is written in the manuscript "Heywood," and the second was doubtless intended for Mrs. Thomas. But in this case the very catholicity of Pope's malice defeated its own aim. Originally the first line stood: "See Pix and slip-shod W—— (Wortley?) traipse along." In 1729 the place of the abused Corinna was given to Mrs. Centlivre, then five years dead, in retaliation for a verse satire called "The Catholic Poet, or Protestant Barnaby's Sorrowful Lamentation: a Ballad about Homer's Iliad," (1715).[12] Evidently abuse equally applicable to anyone or more of five women writers could not be either specific or strikingly personal. Nothing can be inferred from the lines except that Pope despised the whole race of female wits and bore particular malice against certain of their number. Eliza Haywood sustained the largest share of anathema, for not only was she vilified in the poem, but "Haywood's Novels" and the offensive "Court of Carimania" occupied a conspicuous position in the cargo of books carried by the "ass laden with authors" which formed the well-known vignette to the quarto edition of 1729.

In the universal howl raised against the persecutor by the afflicted dunces the treble part was but weakly sustained. Mrs. Thomas indeed produced a small sixpenny octavo, written for, and perhaps in conjunction with Curll, entitled "Codrus; or the Dunciad dissected. To which is added Farmer Pope and his Son" (1729), but Mrs. Haywood's contribution was probably on her part unintentional, and was due entirely to the activity of the same infamous bookseller, who was among the first to get his replies and counter-slanders into print.[13] The "Key to the Dunciad" already mentioned ran through three editions in competition with an authorized key. "The Popiad" and "The Curliad" were rapidly huddled together and placed upon the market. Close upon

---

11. Elwin and Courthope's *Pope*, IV, 294.

12. Elwin and Courthope's *Pope*, IV, 232. See also 159, note I.

13. T.E. Lounsbury, *The Text of Shakespeare*, 281. "'The Popiad' which appeared in July, and 'The Female Dunciad' which followed the month after. . . were essentially miscellanies devoted to attacks upon the poet, and for them authors were not so much responsible as publishers."

the heels of these publications came "The Female Dunciad," containing beside the "Metamorphosis of P. into a Stinging Nettle" by Mr. Foxton, a novel called "Irish Artifice; or, the History of Clarina" by Mrs. Eliza Haywood. In a short introduction to the piece, Curll explained how it happened to fall into his hands.

> "I am likewise to inform my *Female Criticks*, that they stand indebted to the entertaining Pen of Mrs. *Eliza Haywood* for the following *History* of Clarina. It was sent to me, by herself, on communicating to some of my Friends the Design I had of writing a Weekly Paper, under the title of the ROVER, the Scope of which is in some Measure explain'd in her Address to me, and this Project I may yet perhaps put in Execution."

The novelette submitted to Curll for inclusion in his projected periodical relates how an Irish housekeeper named Aglaura craftily promotes a runaway match between her son Merovius and the young heiress Clarina, who, deserted by her husband and disowned by her father, falls into the utmost misery. The story has no possible bearing either on Pope or on "The Dunciad," but was evidently seized by the shifty publisher as the nearest thing to hand when he came to patch up another pamphlet against Pope. Nothing could be more characteristic of Curll than his willingness to make capital out of his own disgrace. So hurried was the compilation of "The Female Dunciad" that he even printed the letter designed to introduce Mrs. Haywood's tale to the readers of the "Rover." Pope, who assiduously read all the libels directed against himself, hastened to use the writer's confession of her own shortcomings in a note to "The Dunciad, Variorum" of 1729.[14]

Mrs. Haywood admires at some length the Rover's intention of "laying a Foundation for a Fabrick, whose spacious Circumference shall at once display the beautiful Images of Virtue in in all her proper Shapes, and the Deformities of Vice in its various Appearances. . . An Endeavour for a Reformation of Manners, (in an Age, where Folly is so much the Fashion, that to have run thro' all the courses of Debauchery, seem requisite to complete the fine Gentleman) is an Attempt as *daring* as it is *noble*; and while it engages the Admiration and Applause of the worthy and judicious *Few*, will certainly draw on you the Ridicule

---

14. Elwin and Courthope's *Pope*, IV, 141, note 5.

and Hatred of that *unnumber'd Crowd*, who justly dread the Lash of a Satire, which their own dissolute Behaviour has given sting to. But I, who am perfectly acquainted with the Sweetness of your Disposition, and that Tenderness with which you consider the Errors of your Fellow Creatures, need not be inform'd, that while you expose the Foulness of those Facts, which renders them deservedly Objects of Reproach, you will (not) forget to pity the Weakness of Humanity and Lethargy of Reason, which at some unguarded Hours, steals on the Souls of even the wisest Men; and tho' I shou'd find, in the Course of your Papers, all the little Inadvertencies of my own Life recorded, I am sensible it will be done in such a Manner as I cannot but approve."

No particular intimacy between the author and the bookseller can be inferred from this extravagant but conventional flattery. The interpretation of what Mrs. Haywood terms inadvertencies—a word almost invariably used in her writings as a euphemism—is a more difficult problem, for definite evidence of the authoress' gallantries is entirely lacking. But however damaging to herself her frankness may have been, there was little in the production to arouse the ire of Pope. The only instance in which the maligned novelist may have intended to show her resentment was in the Preface to her tragedy "Frederick, Duke of Brunswick-Lunenburgh" (1729) where with veiled sarcasm she confessed herself "below the Censure of the Gyant-Criticks of this Age."

Although Mrs. Haywood was evidently not responsible for the inclusion of her tale in "The Female Dunciad," and although the piece itself was entirely innocuous, her daring to raise her head even by accident brought down upon her another scurrilous rebuke, not this time from the poet himself, but from her former admirer, Richard Savage. In "An Author to be Let" (1732) Pope's jackal directed against the members of a supposed club of dunces, presided over by James Moore-Smith and including Theobald, Welsted, Curll, Dennis, Cooke, and Bezaleel Morris, a tirade of abuse, in which "the divine Eliza" came in for her full share of vituperation.

"When Mrs. Haywood ceas'd to be a Strolling Actress, why might not the Lady (tho' once a Theatrical Queen) have subsisted by turning Washer-woman? Has not the Fall of Greatness been a frequent Distress in all Ages? She might have caught a beautiful Bubble as it arose from the Suds of her Tub, blown it in Air, seen it glitter, and then break! Even in this low Condition, she had play'd with a Bubble, and what more, is the Vanity of human Greatness? She might also have consider'd the sullied Linnen growing white in her pretty red Hands, as an Emblem of her Soul, were it well scoured by Repentance for the Sins of her Youth: But she rather chooses starving by writing Novels of Intrigue, to teach young Heiresses the Art of running away with Fortune-hunters, and scandalizing Persons of the highest Worth and Distinction."

Savage's mention of eloping heiresses shows that he had been looking for exceptionable material in "Irish Artifice," but finding little to his purpose there, had reverted to the stock objections to the scandal novels, where he was upon safe but not original ground. In the body of the pamphlet he returned to assault the same breach. The supposed writer, Iscariot Hackney, in stating his qualifications for membership in the Dunces' Club, claims to be "very deeply read in all Pieces of Scandal, Obscenity, and Prophaneness, particularly in the Writings of Mrs. *Haywood, Henley, Welsted, Morley, Foxton, Cooke, D'Foe, Norton, Woolston, Dennis, Nedward, Concanen, Journalist-Pit*, and the Author of the *Rival Modes*. From these I propose to compile a very grand Work, which shall not be inferior to *Utopia, Carimania, Guttiverania, Art of Flogging, Daily Journal*, Epigrams on the *Dunciad*, or *Oratory Transactions*." . . . Although the author of "Utopia" and "Carimania" was pilloried in good company, she suffered more than she deserved. She was indeed a friend of Theobald's, for a copy of "The Dunciad: with Notes Variorum, and the Prolegomena of Scriblerus," bearing on the fly-leaf the following inscription:

"Lewis Theobald to Mrs Heywood, as a testimony of his esteem, presents this book called *The Dunciad*, and acquaints her that Mr. Pope, by the profits of its publication, saved his library, *wherein unpawned much learned lumber lay*."[15]

shows that the two victims of Pope's most bitter satire felt a sort of companionship in misfortune. But there is no evidence to show that Eliza took any part in the War of the Dunces.

---

15. Notes and Queries, Ser. I, X, 110. The words italicized by me refer to Pope's description of Theobald's library, *The Dunciad*, (1728), Book I, line 106.

But that the immortal infamy heaped upon her by "The Dunciad" injured her prospects cannot be doubted. She was far from being a "signal illustration of the powerlessness of this attack upon the immediate fortunes of those assailed," as Professor Lounsbury describes her.[16] It is true that she continued to write, though with less frequency than before, and that some of her best-sellers were produced at a time when Pope's influence was at its height, but that the author was obliged to take extreme measures to avoid the ill consequences of the lampoon upon her may be proved by comparing the title-pages of her earlier and later novels.

Before the publication of "The Dunciad" the adventuress in letters had enjoyed a large share of popularity. Most of her legitimate works were advertised as "Written by Mrs. Eliza Haywood" and bore her name in full prominently displayed on the title-page. That her signature possessed a distinct commercial value in selling popular fiction was amusingly illustrated by a bit of literary rascality practiced in 1727, when Arthur Bettesworth, the bookseller, issued a chapbook called "The Pleasant and Delightful History of Gillian of Croydon." After a long summary of the contents in small type came the statement, "The Whole done much after the same Method as those celebrated Novels, By Mrs. ELIZA HAYWOOD," the forged author's name being emphasized in the largest possible type in the hope that a cursory glance at the title-page might deceive a prospective buyer.[17] Of her forty publications before 1728 only fifteen, of which five from their libelous nature could not be acknowledged, failed to sail openly under her colors. Only once did she employ any sort of pseudonym, and only in one case was her signature relegated to the end of the dedication.[18] A word of scorn from the literary dictator, however, was enough to turn the taste of

---

16. T. R. Lounsbury, *The Text of Shakespeare*, 275. "But the attack upon Mrs. Haywood exceeded all bounds of decency. To the credit of the English race nothing so dastardly and vulgar can be found elsewhere in English literature. If the influence of 'The Dunciad' was so all-powerful as to ruin the prospects of anyone it satirized, it ought certainly to have crushed her beyond hope of any revival. As a matter of fact Mrs. Haywood's most successful and popular writings were produced after the publication of that poem, and that too at a period when Pope's predominance was far higher than it was at the time the satire itself appeared."

17. A. Esdaile, *English Tales and Romances*, Introduction, xxviii.

18. *The Mercenary Lover. . . Written by the Author of Memoirs of the said Island* (Utopia) and described on the half-title as by E. H. and *The Fair Captive*, a tragedy not originally written by her.

the town, not indeed away from sensational and scandalous fictions, but away from the hitherto popular writer of them. Eliza Haywood was no longer a name to conjure with; her reputation was irretrievably gone. It was no unusual thing in those days for ladies in semi-public life to outlive several reputations. The quondam Clio had already found the notoriety of that name too strong for her comfort, and had been rechristened Mira by the dapper Mr. Mallet.[19] Instead of adopting some such expedient Mrs. Haywood found it more convenient simply to lapse into anonymity. Of the four novels published within a year after "The Dunciad" none bore her name on the title-page, though two had signed dedications and the others were advertised as by her. Not one of them was re-issued. The tragedy "Frederick, Duke of Brunswick-Lunenburgh," known to be of her make, was a complete failure, and "Love-Letters on All Occasions" (1730) with "Collected by Mrs. Eliza Haywood" on the title-page never reached a second edition. Both her translations from the French, "L'Entretien des Beaux Esprits" (1734) and "The Virtuous Villager" (1742), were acknowledged at the end of the dedications, and both were unsuccessful, although the anonymous predecessor of the former, "La Belle Assemblee" (1725), ran through eight editions. The single occurrence of Mrs. Haywood's name on a title-page after 1730, if we except the two reprints of "Secret Histories," was when the unacknowledged "Adventures of Eovaai" (1736) re-appeared five years later as "The Unfortunate Princess" with what seems to be a "fubbed" title-page for which the author was probably not responsible. And the successful works referred to by Professor Lounsbury were all either issued without any signature or under such designations as "the Author of the Fortunate Foundlings," or "Mira, one of the Authors of the Female Spectator," or "Exploralibus," so that even the reviewers sometimes appeared to be ignorant of the writer's identity.

Moreover, Mrs. Haywood's re-establishment as an anonymous author seems to have been a work of some difficulty, necessitating a ten years' struggle against adversity. Between 1731 and 1741 she produced fewer books than during any single year of her activity after the publication of "Idalia" and before "The Dunciad." Her probable share

---

19. *Philobillon Soc. Misc.*, IV, 12. "Clio must be allowed to be a most complete poetess, if she really wrote those poems that bear her name; but it has of late been so abused and scandalized, that I am informed she has lately changed it for that of Myra." Quoted from the *British Journal*, 24 September, 1726. I am indebted to Miss Dorothy Brewster's *Aaron Hill*, 189, for this reference.

in the "Secret Memoirs of Mr. Duncan Campbel" was merely that of a hack writer, her contributions to the "Opera of Operas" were of the most trifling nature, and the two volumes of "L'Entretien des Beaux Esprits" were not original. For six years after the "Adventures of Eovaai" she sent to press no work now known to be hers, and not until the catch-penny "Present for a Servant-Maid" (1743) and the anonymous "Fortunate Foundlings" (1744) did her wares again attain the popularity of several editions. All due credit must be allowed Mrs. Haywood for her persistent efforts to regain her footing as a woman of letters, for during this time she had little encouragement. Pope's attack did destroy her best asset, her growing reputation as an author, but instead of following Savage's ill-natured advice to turn washerwoman, she remained loyal to her profession and in her later novels gained greater success than she had ever before enjoyed. But it was only her dexterity that saved her from literary annihilation.[20]

The lesson of her hard usage at the hands of Pope and his allies, however, was not lost upon the adaptable dame. After her years of silence Mrs. Haywood seems to have returned to the production of perishable literature with less inclination for gallantry than she had evinced in her early romances. Warm-blooded creature though she was, Eliza could not be insensible to the cooling effect of age, and perhaps, too, she perceived the more sober moral taste of the new generation. "In the numerous volumes which she gave to the world towards the latter part of her life," says the "Biographia Dramatica," somewhat hastily, "no author has appeared more the votary of virtue, nor are there any novels in which a stricter purity, or a greater delicacy of sentiment, has been preserved." Without discussing here the comparative decency of Mrs. Haywood's later novels, we may admit at once, with few

---

20. See Clara Reeve, *The Progress of Romance* (1785), I, 121. (I have re-arranged the passage for the sake of brevity.)

"*Soph.* I have heard it often said that Mr. Pope was too severe in his treatment of this lady: it was supposed that she had given some private offence, which he resented publicly, as was too much his way.

"*Euph.* Mr. Pope was severe in his castigations, but let us be just to merit of every kind. Mrs. *Heywood* had the singular good fortune to recover a lost reputation and the yet greater honour to atone for her errors.—She devoted the remainder of her life and labours to the service of virtue. . . Those works by which she is most likely to be known to posterity, are the *Female Spectator*, and the *Invisible Spy*. . ."

GEORGE WHICHER

allowances for change of standard, the moral excellence of such works as "The Female Spectator" and "Epistles for the Ladies." Certainly if the penance paid by the reader is any test, the novelist was successful in her effort to atone for the looseness of her early writings, when she left the province of fiction for that of the periodical essay.

VI

Letters and Essays

The works of Mrs. Haywood's maturity most renowned for their pious intent were not of the tribe of novels, but rather in the shape of letters or periodical essays such as "Epistles for the Ladies" (1749) and "The Female Spectator" (1746). Each of these forms, as practiced during the eighteenth century, permitted the introduction of short romantic stories either for the purpose of illustrating a moral or to make the didacticism more palatable. Even as a votary of virtue Eliza did not neglect to mingle a liberal portion of *dulce* with her *utile*; indeed in the first of the productions mentioned she manifested an occasional tendency to revert to the letter of amorous intrigue characteristic of her earlier efforts. In her latest and soberest writings, the conduct books called "The Wife" and "The Husband" (1756), she frequently yielded to the temptation to turn from dry precept to picturing the foibles of either sex. Her long training in the school of romance had made gallantry the natural object of Eliza Haywood's thoughts.

During the time that she was incessantly occupied with short tales of passion she had experimented in both the letter and the essay form, using the former especially as an adjunct to her stories. One of her first attempts, also, to find her proper vein as an author was a translation from the French of the "Letters from a Lady of Quality to a Chevalier," with a "Discourse concerning Writings of this Nature, by Way of Essay" for which the translator was responsible. In "The Tea-Table" (1725), which never advanced beyond the second part, and "Reflections on the Various Effects of Love" (1726) the then well-known novelist returned to the essay form, and a comprehensive volume of "Love-Letters on All Occasions" (1730) closed the first period of her literary activity. But none of these departures was noticeably different in tone from her staple romances.

The sweets of love were perhaps most convincingly revealed in the amorous billets of which "Love in Excess" and many of Eliza's subsequent pieces of fiction contained a plentiful supply. Letters languishing with various degrees of desire or burning with jealous rage were introduced into the story upon any pretext. Writing them was evidently the author's forte, and perusing them apparently a pleasure to her readers, for they remained a conspicuous part of Mrs. Haywood's sentimental paraphernalia. As in the French romances of the Scudéry type the missives were quoted at length and labeled with such headings as, "The Despairing D'Elmont to his Repenting Charmer," or "To the never enough Admir'd Count D'Elmont," and signed with some such formula as, "Your most passionate and tender, but ('till she receives a favorable Answer) your unknown Adorer." The custom of inserting letters in the course of the story was, as has already been indicated, a heritage from the times of Gomberville, La Calprenède, and the Scudérys when miscellaneous material of all sorts from poetry to prosy conversations was habitually used to diversify the narrative. Mrs. Haywood, however, employed the letter not to ornament but to intensify. Her *billets-doux* like the lyrics in a play represent moments of supreme emotion. In seeking vividness she too often fell into exaggeration, as in the following specimen of absolute passion.

> "Torture—Distraction—Hell—what will become of me—I
> cannot—I will not survive the Knowledge that you are mine
> no more—Yet this Suspence is worse than all yet ever bore
> the Name of Horror—Let me not linger in it, if you have
> Humanity—declare my Doom at once—be kind in Cruelty
> at least, and let one Death conclude the thousand, thousand
> Deaths which every Minute of Uncertainty brings with it, to
> The Miserable, but
Still Adoring
Melantha
>
> P.S. I have order'd the Messenger to bring an Answer; if
> he comes without, depend I will murder him, and then
> myself."[1]

Such remnants of the romantic tradition as the verses on "The Unfortunate Camilla's Complaint to the Moon, for the Absence of her dear Henricus Frankville" in "Love in Excess" were soon discarded, but the letters, though they encumbered the progress of the narrative, made

---

1. *Memoirs of a Certain Island*, I, 141. The letter is one of a packet conveyed away by Sylphs much resembling those in *The Rape of the Lock*.

it more realistic by giving an opportunity for the display of passion at first hand. Their continued vogue was undoubtedly due in large measure to the popularity of the celebrated "Letters of a Portuguese Nun" (1669), which, with a note of sincerity till then unknown, aided the return to naturalness.[2]

The "Lettres Nouvelles de Monsieur Boursault. . . Avec Treize Lettres Amoureuses d'une Dame à un Cavalier," loosely translated by Mrs. Haywood as "Letters from a Lady of Quality to a Chevalier" (1721),[3] was one of the numerous imitations of the Portuguese Letters. Like most of the other imitations it echoed the mannerisms rather than the fervor of its original. The lady's epistles do not reveal a story, but describe in detail the doubts, disappointments, fears, jealousies, and raptures of a married woman for a lover who in the last three letters has left France for England. Except for this remove there is no change in the situation of the characters. The lover apparently remains constant to the end. The reader is even left in some doubt as to the exact nature of their relationship. The lady at one time calls it a "criminal Conversation," but later resents an attempt upon her honor, and seems generally to believe that "a distant Conversation, if it is less sweet, will be, not only more pure, but also more durable."

But perhaps it is only fair to let the author speak for herself.

"The Lady, whose Letters I have taken the liberty to translate, tho she has been cautious enough in expressing anything (even in those the most tender among them) which can give the Reader an Assurance she had forfeited her Virtue; yet there is not one, but what sufficiently proves how impossible it is to maintain such a Correspondence, without an Anxiety and continual Perturbation of Mind, which I think a Woman must have bid farewell to her Understanding, before she could resolve to endure.

"In the very first she plainly discovers the Agitation of her Spirits, confesses she knows herself in the wrong, and that every Expression her Tenderness forces from her, is a Stab to her Peace; she dreads the Effects of her Lover's too powerful Attractions,

---

2. Miss C.E. Morgan, *The Novel of Manners*, 72.
3. The author herself describes it in the Preface as "more properly. . . a Paraphrase than a Translation."

doubts her own Strength of resisting such united Charms as she finds in him, and trembles at the Apprehensions, that by some unlucky Accident the Secret should be known. Everything alarms her. . . 'Tis impossible to be conscious of anything we wish to conceal, without suspecting the most undesigning Words and Actions as Snares laid to entrap us. . . So this unfortunate Lady, divided between Excess of Love, and Nicety of Honour, could neither resolve to give a loose to the one, nor entirely obey the Precepts of the other, but suffered herself to be tossed alternately by both. And tho the Person she loved was most certainly (if such a thing can be) deserving all the Condescensions a Woman could make, by his Assiduity, Constancy, and Gratitude, yet it must be a good while before she could receive those Proofs; and the Disquiets she suffered in that time of Probation, were, I think, if no worse ensued, too dear a Price for the Pleasure of being beloved by the most engaging and most charming of his Sex."

The "Discourse concerning Writings of this Nature," from which the above quotation is taken, makes no attempt to consider other series of amorous letters, but proceeds to enforce by platitudes and scraps of poetry the only too obvious moral of the lady of quality's correspondence. The author remembers how "a Lady of my Acquaintance, perhaps not without reason, fell one day, as she was sitting with me, into this Poetical Exclamation:

> 'The Pen can furrow a fond Female's Heart,
> And pierce it more than Cupid's talk'd-of Dart:
> Letters, a kind of Magick Virtue have,
> And, like strong Philters, human Souls enslave!'"

After thirty pages of moralizing the writer comes to a conclusion with the reflection, a commonplace of her novels, that "if the little I have done, may give occasion to some abler Pen to expose (such indiscretions) more effectually, I shall think myself happy in having given a hint, which improv'd, may be of so general a Service to my Sex." But the impression left by this and others of Mrs. Haywood's works is that the fair novelist was not so much interested in preventing the inadvertencies of her sex as in exposing them.

The tender passion was still the theme in "Love-Letters on All Occasions Lately passed between Persons of Distinction," which contains a number of letters, mainly disconnected, devoted to the warmer phases of gallantry. Some are essays in little on definite subjects: levity, sincerity, the pleasures of conjugal affection, insensibility, and so on. Most of them, however, are occasional: "Strephon to Dalinda, on her forbidding him to speak of Love," "Orontes to Deanira, entreating her to give him a meeting," and many others in which both the proper names and the situations suggest the artificial romances. None of the missives reveals emotions of any but the most tawdry romantic kind, warm desires extravagantly uttered, conventional doubts, causeless jealousies, and petty quarrels. Like Mrs. Behn's correspondence with the amorous Van Bruin these epistles have nothing to distinguish them except their excessive hyperbole. There is one series of twenty-four connected letters on the model of "Letters from a Lady of Quality to a Chevalier," relating the love story of Theano and Elismonda, but in the course of the whole correspondence nothing more momentous occurs than the lover's leaving town. Indeed so imperceptible is the narrative element in Mrs. Haywood's epistolary sequences that they can make no claim to share with the anonymous love story in letters entitled "Love's Posy" (1686), with the "Letters Written By Mrs. Manley" (1696),[4] or with Tom Brown's "Adventures of Lindamira" (1702) in twenty-four letters, the honor of having anticipated Richardson's method of telling a story in epistolary form.[5]

Even after the publication of "Pamela" and "Clarissa" Mrs. Haywood failed to realize the narrative possibilities of consecutive letters, for "Epistles for the Ladies" (1749) hardly contains three missives on anyone theme. Though the collection is not free from letters in the vein of gallantry, the emphasis on the whole is decidedly changed. There are few attempts to exploit the emotions by describing the palpitations of injured beauty or the expostulations and vows of love-sick cavaliers. Instead Aminta is praised for enduring with unusual self-possession the treachery of her lover and her most intimate friend. Sophronia encourages Palmira to persist in her resolution of living apart from her husband until she is convinced of the reformation of his manners, and Isabinda sends to Elvira a copy of a modest epithalamium on her

4. Later *A Stage-Coach Journey to Exeter*, 1725.
5. A. Esdaile, *English Tales and Romances*, Introduction, xxxiii. B.

sister's marriage. Occasionally a romantic love story runs through three or four letters, but any deviation from the strictest principles of delicacy—and there are not many—is sure to be followed by a fitting catastrophe. Some reprobation of the licentious manners of the age is permitted, but no catering to degenerate taste and no breath of scandal. The aim of the epistles, which were apparently not intended as models, was to convey moral precepts in an agreeably alleviated form, but the balance inclines rather heavily toward sober piety. A mother recommends poetry and history for the reading of her twelve year old daughter, though allowing an occasional indulgence in "well wrote Novels." Eusebia discusses the power of divine music with the Bishop of ***. Berinthia writes to Berenice to urge her to make the necessary preparations for futurity. Philenia assures the Reverend Doctor *** that she is a true penitent, and beseeches his assistance to strengthen her pious resolutions. Hillaria laments to Clio that she is unable to think seriously on death, and Aristander edifies Melissa by proving from the principles of reason and philosophy the certainty of a future existence, and the absurdity and meanness of those people's notions, who degrade the dignity of their species, and put human nature on a level with that of the brute creation. In all this devotion there was no doubt something of Mrs. Howe. "Epistles for the Ladies" was not the first "attempt to employ the ornaments of romance in the decoration of religion"[6] nor the best, but along with the pious substance the author sometimes adopts an almost Johnsonian weightiness of style, as when Ciamara gives to Sophronia an account of the finishing of a fine building she had been at an infinite expense in erecting, with some moral reflections on the vanity and disappointment of all sub-lunary expectations.

In her essays, even the most serious, Mrs. Haywood was a follower of Addison rather than Johnson. The first of them, if we disregard the slight discourse appended to the "Letters from a Lady of Quality to a Chevalier," was "The Tea-Table: or, A Conversation between some Polite Persons of both Sexes, at a Lady's Visiting Day. Wherein are represented the Various Foibles, and Affectations, which form the Character of an Accomplish'd Beau, or Modern Fine Lady. Interspersed with several Entertaining and Instructive Stories,"[7] (1725), which most resembles

---

6. Robert Boyle's *Martyrdom of Theodora*, 1687, is thus described by Dr. Johnson. Boswell's *Johnson*, Oxford ed., I, 208.

7. Not to be confused with a periodical entitled *The Tea-Table. To be continued every Monday and Friday*. No. 1–36, 21 February to 22 June, 1724. B.M. (P.P. 5306).

a "day" detached from the interminable "La Belle Assemblée" of Mme de Gomez, translated by Mrs. Haywood a few months before. There is the same polite conversation, the debate between love and reason, the poem,[8] and the story. But the moral reflections upon tea-tables, the description of Amiana's, where only wit and good humor prevail, and the satirical portraits of a titled coxcomb and a bevy of fine ladies, are all in the manner of the "Tatler." The manuscript novel read by one of the company savors of nothing but Mrs. Haywood, who was evidently unable to slight her favorite theme of passion. Her comment on contemporary manners soon gives place to "Beraldus and Celemena: or the Punishment of Mutability," a tale of court intrigue in her warmest vein. The authors of the "Tatler" and "Spectator" had, of course, set a precedent for the inclusion of short romantic stories in the essay of manners, and even the essays with no distinct element of fiction were preparing for the novelist the powerful tool of characterization. Writers of fiction were slow to apply the new art to their proper materials. In the present instance an experienced novelist employed the essay form to depict the follies and affectations of a beau and fine ladies, and immediately turned back to a story in which characterization is almost entirely neglected for incident. It is interesting to find the same writer using the realistic sketch of manners and the romantic tale of intrigue and passion without any thought of combining the two elements. In the second part of "The Tea-Table" Mrs. Haywood made no attempt to diversify the patchwork of verse and prose with any narrative, save one small incident illustrating pride. The sole point of interest is the long and laudatory tribute to her friend Aaron Hill in "A Pastoral Dialogue, between Alexis and Clarinda; Occasioned by Hillarius's intending a Voyage to America."

The "Reflections on the Various Effects of Love" (1726), however, takes full advantage of the looseness of the essay form to become a mere tissue of short narratives illustrating the consequences of passion. The stories of Celia and Evandra, one cursing her betrayer, the other wishing him always happy, exemplify revengeful and generous love. There are two model epistles from Climene to Mirtillo, the first upon his absence, the second upon his desertion of her. Soon the trite remarks degenerate into a scandal novel, relating the history of Sophiana, abandoned by

---

8. *Ximene fearing to be forsaken by Palemon, desires he would kill her.* Quoted by Dyce, *Specimens of British Poetesses*, 1827, p. 186.

Aranthus and sought by Martius, with many of her letters describing her gradual change of heart in favor of the beseeching lover. In the midst of exposing Hibonio's sudden infatuation for a gutter-nymph, the essay abruptly ends with the exclamation, "More of this in our next." Though there was no lack of slander at the end of Mrs. Haywood's pen, she never attempted to continue the "Reflections."

But almost twenty years later she made a more noteworthy excursion into the field of the periodical essay. "The Female Spectator," begun in April, 1744, and continued in monthly parts until May, 1746, bid fair to become the best known and most approved of her works. The twenty-four numbers (two months being omitted) were bound in four volumes upon the completion of the series and sold with such vigor that an edition labeled the third was issued at Dublin in 1747. In 1771 the seventh and last English edition was printed. As in the original "Spectator" the essays are supposed to be the product of a Club, in this case composed of four women. After drawing her own character in the terms already quoted,[9] Mrs. Haywood mentions as her coadjutors in the enterprise "Mira, a Lady descended from a Family to which Wit seems hereditary, married to a Gentleman every way worthy of so excellent a Wife. . . The next is a Widow of Quality" who has not "buried her Vivacity in the Tomb of her Lord. . . The Third is the Daughter of a wealthy Merchant, charming as an Angel. . . This fine young Creature I shall call Euphrosine." The suspiciously representative character of these assistants may well make us doubt their actuality; and from the style of the lucubrations, at least, no evidence of a plurality of authors can readily be perceived. Indeed after the first few numbers we hear nothing more of them. "Mira" was the pseudonym used by Mrs. Haywood in "The Wife" (1756), while a periodical called "The Young Lady" began to appear just before her death under the pen-name of Euphrosine.

Whether written by a Female Spectator Club or by a single authoress, the essays in purpose, method, and style are evidently imitated from their famous model. The loose plan and general intention to rectify the manners of the age allowed the greatest latitude in the choice of subject matter. In a single paper are jumbled together topics so diverse as the degradation of the stage, the immoderate use of tea, and the proper choice of lovers. The duty of periodical essayists to castigate the follies

9. See *ante*, p. 24.

of the time is graphically represented in the frontispiece to the second volume, where Apollo, seated on some substantial clouds and holding in his hand "The Female Spectator," despatches a flying Mercury, who in spite of the efforts of two beaux with drawn swords and a belle in *déshabillé*, chastises a female figure of Luxuria lolling in a chariot pulled by one inadequate grasshopper. In the essays themselves the same purpose led to the censure of gambling, lying, affectation of youth by the aged, jilts, "Anti-Eternitarians," scandal bearing, and other petty sins and sinners. For political readers a gentleman contributes a conversation between a Hanoverian and an English lady, in which the latter has the best of the argument. An account of Topsy-Turvy Land satirizes illogical practices in a manner familiar to the readers of "The Bab Ballads." The few literary papers are concerned with true and false taste, the delights of reading, Mr. Akenside's "Pleasures of the Imagination" and the horrors of the same, the outwearing of romance, and love-letters passed between Augustus Caesar and Livia Drusilla, which last Mrs. Haywood was qualified to judge as an expert. Essays on religion and the future life reveal something of the sober touch and moral earnestness of Johnson, but nothing of his compact and weighty style. As in the "Spectator," topics are often introduced by a scrap of conversation by way of a text or by a letter from a correspondent setting forth some particular grievance. The discussion is frequently illustrated by anecdotes or even by stories, though the author makes comparatively small use of her talent for fiction. Indeed she records at one point that "Many of the Subscribers to this Undertaking. . . complain that. . . I moralize too much, and that I give them too few Tales." The Oriental setting used by Addison with signal success is never attempted and even scandal stories are frowned upon. Instead of the elaborate and elegantly turned illustrative narratives of the "Spectator," Mrs. Haywood generally relates anecdotes which in spite of the disguised names savor of crude realism. They are examples rather than illustrations of life.

One of the most lively is a story told to show the inevitable unhappiness of a marriage between persons of different sects. The husband, a High Church man, and the wife, of Presbyterian persuasion, were happy enough during the first months of married life, "tho' he sometimes expressed a Dissatisfaction at being denied the Pleasure of leading her to Westminster-Abbey, for he would hear no Divine Service out of a Cathedral, and she was no less troubled that she could not prevail with him to make his Appearance with her at the Conventicle."

Consequently when their first child was born, they were unable to agree how the boy was to be baptized. "All their Discourse was larded with the most piquant Reflections," but to no purpose. The father insisted upon having his own way, but Amonia, as his consort was not inappropriately named, was no less stubborn in her detestation of lawn sleeves, and on the eve of the christening had the ceremony privately performed by her own minister. When the bishop and the guests were assembled, she announced with "splenetic Satisfaction" that the child had already been "made a Christian" and that his name was John. The astonished husband lapsed into an "adequate rage," and though restrained by the company from doing an immediate violence to his help-mate, was permanently estranged from her through his resentment. Two other stories from "The Female Spectator" were quoted by Dr. Nathan Drake in his "Gleaner."

In her bold attempt to rival Addison upon his own ground Mrs. Haywood was more than moderately successful in the estimation of many of her contemporaries. Rambling and trite as are the essays in her periodical, their excellent intentions, at least, gained them a degree of popularity. A writer in the "Gentleman's Magazine" for December, 1744, applauding the conspicuous merit of the "fair philosophers in virtue's cause," declared that

> *"Were your great predecessor yet on earth,*
> *He'd be the first to speak your page's worth,*
> *There all the foibles of the fair you trace;*
> *There do you shew your sex's truest grace;*
> *There are the various wiles of man display'd,*
> *In gentle warnings to the cred'lous maid;*
> *Politely pictur'd, wrote with strength and ease,*
> *And while the wand'rer you reclaim, you please. . .*
> *Women, the heart of women best can reach;*
> *While men from maxims—you from practice teach."*

The latter part of the panegyric shows that the fair romancer had not been entirely smothered in the fair philosopher and moral essayist.

Perhaps encouraged by the success of "The Female Spectator" to publish more frequently, or actuated by a desire to appeal to the public interest in the political excitement of 1745–6, Mrs. Haywood next attempted to combine the periodical essay with the news-letter, but the innovation evidently failed to please. "The Parrot, with a Compendium of the Times" ran only from 2 August to 4 October, 1746. The numbers consisted commonly of two parts: the first being moralizings on life and manners by a miraculous parrot; and the second a digest of whatever happenings the author could scrape together. The news of the day was concerned chiefly with the fate of the rebels in the last Stuart uprising and with rumors of the Pretender's movements. From many indications Eliza Haywood would seem to have taken a lively interest in the Stuart cause, but certainly she had no exceptional facilities for reporting the course of events, and consequently her budget of information was often stale or filled with vague surmises. But she did not overlook the opportunity to narrate *con amore* such pathetic incidents as the death of Jemmy Dawson's sweetheart at the moment of his execution, later the subject of Shenstone's ballad. The vaporizings of the parrot were also largely inspired by the trials of the rebels, but the sagacious bird frequently drew upon such stock subjects as the follies of the gay world, the character of women, the unreliability of venal praise and interested personal satire, and the advantages of making one's will—the latter illustrated by a story. Somewhat more unusual was a letter from an American Poll, representing how much it was to the interest of England to preserve, protect, and encourage her plantations in the New World, and complaining of the tyranny of arbitrary governors. But the essay parts of "The Parrot" are not even equal to "The Female Spectator" and deserve no lightening of the deep and speedy oblivion cast upon them.

Besides her periodical essays Mrs. Haywood wrote during her declining years several conduct books, which, beyond showing the adaptability of her pen to any species of writing, have but small importance. One of them, though inheriting something from Defoe, owed most to the interest in the servant girl heroine excited by Richardson's first novel. No sociologist has yet made a study of the effect of "Pamela" upon the condition of domestics, but the many excellent maxims on the servant question uttered by Lord B—— and his lady can hardly have been without influence upon the persons of the first quality who pored over the volumes. In popular novels, at any rate, abigails and scullions reigned supreme. In 1752 the "Monthly Review" remarked of a recent work of fiction, "The History of Betty Barnes," that it seemed "chiefly calculated for the amusement of a class of people, to whom the *Apprentice's Monitor*, or the *Present for a servant maid* might be recommended to much better purpose," but the reviewer's censure failed to quell the demand for romances of the kitchen. Mrs. Haywood, however, might have approved of his recommendation, since she happened to be the author of the little manual of household science especially urged upon the females below stairs.

"A Present for a Servant-Maid. Or, the Sure Means of Gaining Love and Esteem" was frequently reprinted both in London and Dublin during the years 1743–4, and as late as 1772 a revision was mentioned in the "Monthly Review" as a "well-designed and valuable tract."[10] The work is a compendium of instructions for possible Pamelas, teaching them in brief how to wash, to market, to dress any sort of meat, to cook, to pickle, and to preserve their virtue. The maids are cautioned against such female errors as sluttishness, tale-bearing, staying on errands, telling family affairs, aping the fashion, and giving saucy answers. They are forbidden to play with fire or candles, to quarrel with fellow domestics, to waste victuals or to give them away. A fine example of the morality of scruples inculcated by the tract is the passage on the duty of religious observance. A maidservant should not neglect to go to church at least every other Sunday, and should never spend the time allowed her for that purpose walking in the fields or drinking tea with an acquaintance. "Never say you have been at Church unless you have, but if you have gone out with that Intention, and been diverted from it by any Accident or Persuasions, confess the Truth, if asked." Girls so unhappy as to live with people who "have no Devotion themselves" should entreat permission to go to church, and if it is refused them, rather leave their place than be deprived of sacred consolation. "If you lose *one*, that God, for whose sake you have left it, will doubtless provide another, and perhaps a better for you." Scarcely more edifying are the considerations of self-interest which should guide a maidservant into the paths of virtue. "Industry and Frugality are two very amiable Parts of a Woman's Character, and I know no readier Way than attaining them, to procure you the Esteem of Mankind, and get yourselves good Husbands. Consider, my dear Girls, that you have no Portions, and endeavour to supply the Deficiencies of Fortune by Mind." And in pure Pamela vein is the advice offered to those maids whose honor is assailed. If the temptation come from the master, it will be well to reflect whether he is a single or a married man and act accordingly. One cannot expect the master's son to keep a promise of marriage without great difficulty,

---

10. *Monthly Review*, XLVI, 463. April, 1772.

but the case may be different with a gentleman lodger, especially if he be old and doting. And the moral of all is: Don't sell yourselves too cheap. Finally to complete the usefulness of the pamphlet were added, "Directions for going to Market: Also, for Dressing any Common Dish, whether Flesh, Fish or Fowl. With some Rules for Washing, &c. The whole calculated for making both the Mistress and the Maid happy."

More especially intended to promote the happiness of the mistress of the family, "The Wife, by Mira, One of the Authors of the Female Spectator, and Epistles for Ladies" (1756) contains advice to married women on how to behave toward their husbands in every conceivable situation, beginning with the first few weeks after marriage "vulgarly call'd the honey-moon," and ending with "How a Woman ought to behave when in a state of Separation from her Husband"—a subject upon which Mrs. Haywood could speak from first-hand knowledge. Indeed it must be confessed that the writer seems to be chiefly interested in the infelicities of married life, and continually alleviates the rigor of her didactic pasages with lively pictures of domestic jars, such as the following:

> "The happy day which had join'd this pair was scarce six weeks elapsed, when lo! behold a most terrible reverse;—the hurry of their fond passion was over;—dalliance was no more,—kisses and embraces were now succeeded by fighting, scratching, and endeavouring to tear out each other's eyes;—the lips that before could utter only,—my dear,—my life,—my soul,—my treasure, now pour'd forth nothing but invectives;—they took as little care to conceal the proofs of their animosity as they had done to moderate those of a contrary emotion;—they were continually quarreling;—their house was a Babel of confusion;—no servant would stay with them a week;—they were shunn'd by their most intimate friends, and despis'd by all their acquaintance; till at last they mutually resolv'd to agree in one point, which was, to be separated forever from each other" (p. 16).

So the author discusses a wife's behavior toward a husband when laboring under disappointment or vexatious accidents; sleeping in different beds; how a woman should act when finding that her husband harbors unjust suspicions of her virtue; the great indiscretion of taking too much notice of the unmeaning or transient gallantries of a husband;

the methods which a wife is justified to take after supporting for a long time a complication of all manner of ill-usage from a husband; and other causes or effects of marital infelicity. Though marriage almost inevitably terminates in a "brulée," the wife should spare no efforts to ameliorate her husband's faults.

"If addicted to drinking, she must take care to have his cellar well stor'd with the best and richest wines, and never seem averse to any company he shall think fit to entertain:—If fond of women, she must endeavour to convince him that the virtuous part of the sex are capable of being as agreeable companions as those of the most loose principles;—and this, not by arguments, for those he will not listen to;—but by getting often to her house, the most witty, gay, and spirituous of her acquaintance, who will sing, dance, tell pleasant stories, and take all the freedoms that innocence allows" (p. 163).

Occasionally the advice to married women is very practical, as the following deterrent from gluttony shows:

"I dined one day with a lady, who the whole time she employ'd her knife and fork with incredible swiftness in dispatching a load of turkey and chine she had heap'd upon her plate, still kept a keen regard on what she had left behind, greedily devouring with her eyes all that remain'd in the dish, and throwing a look of envy on everyone who put in for the smallest share.—My advice to such a one is, that she would have a great looking-glass fix'd opposite the seat she takes at table; and I am much mistaken, if the sight of herself in those grim attitudes I have mention'd, will not very much contribute to bring her to more moderation" (p. 276).

The method of "The Husband, in Answer to the Wife" (1756) is similar to that of its companion-piece; in fact, much of the same advice is merely modified or amplified to suit the other sex. The husband is warned to avoid drinking to excess and someother particulars which may happen to be displeasing to his spouse, such as using too much freedom in his wife's presence with any of her female acquaintance. He is instructed in the manner in which it will be most proper for a married man to carry himself towards the maidservants of his family, and also the manner of behavior best becoming a husband on a full detection of his wife's infidelity. As in "The Wife" the path of marriage leads but to divorce. One is forcibly reminded of Hogarth's "Marriage à la Mode."

Not altogether different is the conception of wedlock in Mrs. Haywood's novels of domestic life written at about the same period, but the pictures there shown are painted in incomparably greater detail, with a fuller appreciation of character, and without that pious didacticism which even the most lively exertions of Eliza Haywood's romancing genius failed to leaven in her essays.

VII

LATER FICTION: THE DOMESTIC NOVEL

No such homogeneity as marked the works of Mrs. Haywood's first decade of authorship can be discovered in the productions of her last fifteen years. The vogue of the short romantic tale was then all but exhausted, her stock of scandal was no longer new, and accordingly she was obliged to grope her way toward fresh fields, even to the barren ground of the moral essay. But besides the letters, essays, and conduct books, and the anonymous pamphlets of doubtful character that may have occupied her pen during this period, she engaged in several experiments in legitimate prose fiction of various sorts, which have little in common except their more considerable length. Although the name of Mrs. Eliza Haywood was not displayed upon the title-pages nor mentioned in the reviews of these novels, the authorship was not carefully concealed and was probably known to the curious. The titles of nearly all of them were mentioned by the "Biographia Dramatica" in the list of the novelist's meritorious works.

The earliest and the only one to bear the signature of Eliza Haywood at the end of the dedication was borrowed from the multifarious and unremarkable literary wares of Charles de Fieux, Chevalier de Mouhy. "The Virtuous Villager, or Virgin's Victory: Being The Memoirs of a very Great Lady at the Court of France. Written by Herself. In which the Artifices of designing Men are fully detected and exposed; and the Calamities they bring on credulous believing Woman, are particularly related," was given to the English public in 1742 as a work suited to inculcate the principles of virtue, and probably owed its being to the previous success of "Pamela."[1] In the original a dull and spiritless imitation of Marivaux, the work was not improved by translation, and met naturally the reception due its slender merits. But along with the English versions of Le Sage, Marivaux, and the Abbé Prévost, "The

---

1. A rival translation called *The Fortunate Countrymaid* had already been published in 1740–1, and may be read in the seventh tome of *The Novelist's Magazine* (Harrison). Clara Reeve speaks of both translations as "well known to the readers of Circulating Libraries." *Progress of Romance* (1785), I, 130.

Virtuous Villager" helped to accustom the readers of fiction to two volume novels and to pave the way for the numerous pages of Richardson.

Not more than a year from the time when the four duodecimos of "Pamela" introduced kitchen morality into the polite world, the generosity of prominent men and women was directed toward a charity recently established after long agitation.[2] To furnish suitable decorations for the Foundling Hospital in Lamb's Conduit, Hogarth contributed the unsold lottery tickets for his "March to Finchley," and other well-known painters lent their services. Handel, a patron of the institution, gave the organ it still possesses, and society followed the lead of the men of genius. The grounds of the Foundling Hospital became in Georgian days a "fashionable morning lounge." Writers of ephemeral literature were not slow to perceive how the wind lay and to take advantage of the interest aroused by the new foundation. The exposed infant, one of the oldest literary devices, was copiously revived, and during the decade when the Hospital was being constructed mention of foundlings on title-pages became especially common. A pamphlet called "The Political Foundling" was followed by the well-known "Foundling Hospital for Wit and Humour" (1743), by Mrs. Haywood's "Fortunate Foundlings" (1744), by Moore's popular comedy, "The Foundling" (1748), and last and greatest by "The History of Tom Jones, a Foundling" (1749), not to mention "The Female Foundling" (1750).

Eliza Haywood's contribution to foundling literature relates the history of twins, brother and sister, found by a benevolent gentleman named Dorilaus in the memorable year 1688. Louisa is of the tribe of Marianne, Pamela, and Henrietta, nor do her experiences differ materially from the course usually run by such heroines. Reared a model of virtue, she is obliged to fly from the house of her guardian to avoid his importunities. After serving as a milliner's apprentice long enough to demonstrate the inviolability of her principles, she becomes mistress of the rules of politeness at the leading courts of Europe as the companion of the gay Melanthe. Saved from an atrocious rake by an honorable lover, whom she is unwilling to accept because of the humbleness of her station, she takes refuge in a convent where she soon becomes so popular that the abbess lays a plot to induce her to become a nun. But escaping the religious snare, she goes back to Paris to be

---

2. Austin Dobson, *Eighteenth Century Vignettes*, First Series, 44. "Captain Coram's Charity."

GEORGE WHICHER

claimed by Dorilaus as his real daughter. Thus every obstacle to her union with her lover is happily removed.

Horatio, meanwhile, after leaving Westminster School to serve as a volunteer in Flanders, has encountered fewer amorous and more military adventures than usually fell to the lot of Haywoodian heroes. His promising career under Marlborough is terminated when he is taken captive by the French, but he is subsequently released to enter the service of the Chevalier. He then becomes enamored of the beautiful Charlotta de Palfoy, and in the hope of making his fortune equal to hers, resolves to cast his lot with the Swedish monarch. In the Saxon campaign he wins a commission as colonel of horse and a comfortable share of the spoils, but later is taken prisoner by the Russians and condemned to languish in a dungeon at St. Petersburg. After many hardships he makes his way to Paris to be welcomed as a son by Dorilaus and as a husband by his adored Charlotta.

In describing Horatio's martial exploits Mrs. Haywood may well have learned some lessons from the "Memoirs of a Cavalier." The narrative is direct and rapid, and diversified by the mingling of private escapades with history. Too much is made, of course, of the hero's personal relations with Charles XII, but that is a fault which few historical novelists have known how to avoid. The geographical background, as well as the historical setting, is laid out with a precision unusual in her fiction. The whole map of Europe is the scene of action, and the author speaks as one familiar with foreign travel, though her passing references to Paris, Venice, Vienna, and other cities have not the full vigor of the descriptions in "Peregrine Pickle."

From the standpoint of structure, too, "The Fortunate Foundlings" is an improvement over the haphazard plots of Mrs. Haywood's early romances, though the double-barreled story necessitated by twin hero and heroine could hardly be told without awkward interruptions in the sequence of one part of the narrative in order to forward the other. But the author doubtless felt that the reader's interest would be freshened by turning from the amorous adventures of Louisa to the daring deeds of Horatio, while a protagonist of each sex enabled her to exhibit at once examples of both male and female virtue. And in spite of inherent difficulties, she succeeded to some extent in showing an interrelation of plots, as where Dorilaus by going to the north of Ireland to hear the dying confession of the mother of his children, thereby misses Horatio's appeal for a ransom, and thus prevents him from rejoining

Marlborough's standard. But there is nothing like Fielding's ingenious linking of events and careful preparation for the catastrophe, nor did Mrs. Haywood make much out of the hint of unconscious incest and the foundling motif which her book has in common with "Tom Jones." Occasionally also she cannot refrain from inserting a bit of court gossip or an amorous page in her warmest manner, but the number of intercalated stories is small indeed compared to that in a romance like "Love in Excess," and they are usually dismissed in a few paragraphs. Here for the first time the author has shown some ability to subordinate sensational incident to the needs of the main plot.

When Mrs. Haywood's inclination or necessities led her back to the novel four years later, she produced a work upon a still more consistent, if also more artificial plan than any of her previous attempts. "Life's Progress through the Passions: or, the Adventures of Natura" avowedly aims to trace the workings of human emotion. The author's purpose is to examine in "what manner the passions operate in every stage of life, and how far the constitution of the *outward frame* is concerned in the emotions of the *internal faculties*," for actions which we might admire or abhor "would lose much of their *eclat* either way, were the secret springs that give them motion, seen into with the eyes of philosophy and reflection." Natura, a sort of Everyman exposed to the variations of passion, is not the faultless hero of romance, but a mere ordinary mortal. Indeed, the writer declares that she is "an enemy to all *romances, novels*, and whatever carries the air of them. . . and as it is a *real*, not *fictitious* character I am about to present, I think myself obliged. . . to draw him such as he was, not such as some sanguine imaginations might wish him to have been."

The survey of the passions begins with an account of Natura's birth of well-to-do but not extraordinary parents, his mother's death, and his father's second marriage, his attack of the small-pox, his education at Eton, and his boyish love for his little play-mate, Delia. Later he becomes more seriously compromised with a woman of the streets, who lures him into financial engagements. Though locked up by his displeased father, he manages to escape, finds his lady entertaining another gallant, and in despair becomes a regular vagabond. Just as he is about to leave England, his father discovers him and sends him to make the grand tour under a competent tutor.

In Paris the tutor dies, and the young man is left to the exercise of his own discretion. Benighted in a wood, he finds shelter in a monastery of noble ladies, where both the abbess and her sister fall in love with him. After fluctuating between the two, he tries to elope with the sister, is foiled by the abbess, and sets off again upon his travels. In Italy he hears of his father's difficulties and starts for home, but enters the French service instead. He is involved with a nobleman in an attempt to abduct a lady from a nunnery, and would have been tortured had not the jailor's wife eloped with him to England. There he enters Parliament and is about to contract a fortunate marriage when he incautiously defends the Chevalier in conversation, fights a duel, and, although his antagonist is only wounded, he finds his reputation blighted by the stigma of Jacobitism. After a long illness at Vienna where he is pestered by Catholic priests, he recovers his health at Spa, and falls in love with a young English girl. Her parents gladly give their consent, but Maria seems unaccountably averse to the match. And when our hero is assaulted by a jealous footman, he perceives that the lady has fixed her affections on a lower object. Natura on his return to England prospers and marries happily, but his joy is soon destroyed by the death of his father and of his wife in giving birth to a son. Consumed by ambition, the widower then marries the niece of a statesman, only to discover what misery there is in a luxurious and unvirtuous wife.

Natura soon experiences the passions of melancholy, grief, and revenge. His son dies, and his wife's conduct forces him to divorce her. In the hope of preventing his brother from inheriting his estate he is about to marry a healthy country girl when he hears that his brother is dead and that his sister's son is now his heir. Thereupon he buys off his intended bride. At his sister's house he meets a young matron named Charlotte, for whom he long entertains a platonic affection, but finally marries her and has three sons. Thereafter he sinks into a calm and natural decline and dies in his sixty-third year.

> "Thus I have attempted to trace nature in all her mazy windings, and shew life's progress through the passions, from the cradle to the grave.—The various adventures which happened to Natura, I thought, afforded a more ample field, than those of anyone man I ever heard, or read of; and flatter myself, that the reader will find many instances, that may contribute to rectify his own conduct, by pointing out those things which ought to be avoided, or at least most carefully guarded against, and those which are worthy to be improved and imitated."

The obvious and conventional moral ending and the shreds of romance that still adhere to the story need not blind us to its unusual features. Besides insisting upon the necessity for psychological analysis of a sort, the author here for the first time becomes a genuine novelist in the sense that her confessed purpose is to depict the actual conditions of life, not to glorify or idealize them. As Fielding was to do in "Tom Jones," Mrs. Haywood proclaims the mediocrity of her hero as his most remarkable quality. Had she been able to make him more than a lay figure distorted by various passions, she might have produced a real character. Although at times he seems to be in danger of acquiring the romantic faculty of causing every woman he meets to fall in love with him, yet the glamor of his youth is obscured by a peaceful and ordinary old age. Artificial in design and stilted in execution as the work is, it nevertheless marks Eliza Haywood's emancipation from the traditions of the romance.[3]

In "The History of Miss Betsy Thoughtless" (1751) she reached the full fruition of her powers as a novelist. Her heroine, like Natura, is little more than a "humour" character, whose prevailing fault is denoted by her surname.[4] Though not fundamentally vicious, her heedless vanity, inquisitiveness, and vivacity lead her into all sorts of follies and embarrassments upon her first entry into fashionable life in London. Among all the suitors who strive to make an impression upon her heart Mr. Trueworth alone succeeds, but her levity and her disregard of appearances force him to think her unworthy of his attentions. Meanwhile her guardian's wife, Lady Mellasin, has been turned out of the house for an egregious infidelity, and Betsy is left to her own scant

---

3. In one other respect Natura belongs to the new rather than to the old school: he takes genuine delight in the wilder beauties of the landscape. "Whether you climb the craggy mountains or traverse the flowery vale; whether thick woods set limits to the sight, or the wide common yields unbounded prospect; whether the ocean rolls in solemn state before you, or gentle streams run purling by your side, nature in all her different shapes delights. . . The stupendous mountains of the Alps, after the plains and soft embowered recesses of Avignon, gave perhaps a no less grateful sensation to the mind of Natura." Such extraordinary appreciation in an age that regarded mountains as frightful excrescences upon the face of nature, makes the connoisseur of the passions a pioneer of the coming age rather than a survival of the last.

4. J. Ireland and J. Nichols, *Hogarth's Works*, Second Series, 31, note. "Mrs. Haywood's *Betsy Thoughtless* was in Ms entitled *Betsy Careless*; but, from the infamy at that time annexed to the name, had a new baptism." The "inimitable Betsy Careless" is sufficiently immortalized in Fielding's *Amelia*, in Mrs. Charke's *Life*, and in Hogarth's *Marriage à la Mode*, Plate III.

GEORGE WHICHER

discretion. After somewhat annoying her brothers by receiving men at her lodgings, she elects under family pressure to marry a Mr. Munden, who quickly shows himself all that a husband should not be. Eventually she has to abandon him, but demonstrates her wifely devotion by going back to nurse him through his last illness. Mr. Trueworth's mate in the interim has conveniently managed to succumb, his old passion revives, and exactly upon the anniversary of Mr. Munden's death he arrives in a chariot and six to claim the fair widow, whose youthful levity has been chastened by the severe discipline of her unfortunate marriage. Told in an easy and dilatory style and interspersed with the inevitable little histories and impassioned letters, the story attained the conventional bulk of four duodecimo volumes.

As Mr. Austin Dobson has pointed out,[5] Mrs. Haywood's novel is remarkable for its scant allusions to actual places and persons. Once mention is made of an appointment "at General Tatten's bench, opposite Rosamond's pond, in St. James's Park," and once a character refers to Cuper's Gardens, but except for an outburst of unexplained virulence directed against Fielding,[6] there is hardly a thought of the novelist's contemporaries. Here is a change indeed from the method of the *chronique scandaleuse*, and a restraint to be wondered at when we remember the worthies caricatured by so eminent a writer as Smollett. But even more remarkable is the difference of spirit between "Betsy Thoughtless" and Mrs. Haywood's earlier and briefer romances. The young *romancière* who in 1725 could write, "Love is a Topick which I believe few are ignorant of. . . a shady Grove and purling Stream are all Things that's necessary to give us an Idea of the tender Passion,"[7] had in a quarter of a century learned much worldly wisdom, and her heroine

---

5. Austin Dobson, *Eighteenth Century Vignettes*, Third Series, 99.
6. "There were no plays, no operas, no masquerades, no balls, no publick shews, except at the Little Theatre in the Hay Market, then known by the name of F——g's scandal shop, because he frequently exhibited there certain drolls, or, more properly, invectives against the ministry; in doing which it appears extremely probable that he had two views; the one to get money, which he very much wanted, from such as delighted in low humour, and could not distinguish true satire from scurrility; and the other, in the hope of having some post given him by those he had abused, in order to silence his dramatick talent. But it is not my business to point either the merit of that gentleman's performances, or the motives he had for writing them, as the town is perfectly acquainted both with his abilities and success, and has since seen him, with astonishment, wriggle himself into favour, by pretending to cajole those he had not the power to intimidate." *The Novelist's Magazine*, XIII, 23. Quoted by Austin Dobson, *Op. cit.*, 100.
7. Dedication of *The Fatal Secret*.

likewise is too sophisticated to be moved by the style of love-making that warmed the susceptible bosoms of Anadea, Filenia, or Placentia. One of Betsy's suitors, indeed, ventured upon the romantic vein with no very favorable results.

"'The deity of soft desires,' said he, 'flies the confused glare of pomp and public shews;—'tis in the shady bowers, or on the banks of a sweet purling stream, he spreads his downy wings, and wafts his thousand nameless pleasures on the fond—the innocent and the happy pair.'

"He was going on, but she interrupted him with a loud laugh. 'Hold, hold,' cried she; 'was there ever such a romantick description? I wonder how such silly ideas come into your head—"shady bowers! and purling streams!"—Heavens, how insipid! Well' (continued she), 'you may be the Strephon of the woods, if you think fit; but I shall never envy the happiness of the Chloe that accompanies you in these fine recesses. What! to be cooped up like a tame dove, only to coo, and bill, and breed? O, it would be a delicious life, indeed!'"[8]

Thus completely metamorphosed were the heroines of Mrs. Haywood's maturest fiction. Betsy Thoughtless is not even the innocent, lovely, and pliable girl typified in Fielding's Sophia Western. She is eminently hard-headed, inquisitive, and practical, and is justly described by Sir Walter Raleigh as "own cousin to Roderick Random."[9]

Whether she may be considered also the ancestor of Evelina must briefly be considered. Dunlop, who apparently originated the idea that "Betsy Thoughtless" might have suggested the plan of Miss Burney's novel, worked out an elaborate parallel between the plots and some of the chief characters of the two compositions.[10] Both, as he pointed out, begin with the launching of a young girl on the great and busy stage of life in London. Each heroine has much to endure from the vulgar manners of a Lady Mellasin or a Madam Duval, and each is annoyed by the malice and impertinence of a Miss Flora or the Misses Branghton. Through their inexperience in the manners of the world and their

---

8. *The Novelist's Magazine*, XIII, 106. Quoted by W. Forsyth, *Novels and Novelists of the Eighteenth Century* (1871), 211.

9. W. Raleigh, *The English Novel* (Fifth edition, 1910), 139.

10. J.C. Dunlop, *History of Prose Fiction*, edited by H. Wilson, II, 568.

heedlessness or ignorance of ceremony both young ladies are mortified by falling into embarrassing and awkward predicaments. Both in the same way alarm the delicacy and almost alienate the affections of their chosen lovers. "The chief perplexity of Mr. Trueworth, the admirer of Miss Thoughtless, arose from meeting her in company with Miss Forward, who had been her companion at a boarding-school, and of whose infamous character she was ignorant. In like manner the delicacy of Lord Orville is wounded, and his attachment shaken, by meeting his Evelina in similar society at Vauxhall. The subsequent visit and counsel of the lovers to their mistresses is seen, however, in a very different point of view by the heroines." The likeness between the plots of the two novels is indeed sufficiently striking to attract the attention of an experienced hunter for literary parallels, but unfortunately there is no external evidence to show that Miss Burney ever read her predecessor's work. One need only compare any two parallel characters, the common profligate, Lady Mellasin, for instance, with the delightfully coarse Madam Duval, to see how little the author of "Evelina" could have learned from the pages of Mrs. Haywood.

But if it deserves scant credit as a model for Miss Burney's infinitely more delicate art, "Betsy Thoughtless" should still be noticed as an early attempt to use the substance of everyday life as material for fiction. It has been called with some justice the first domestic novel in the language. Although the exact definition of a domestic novel nowhere appears, the term may be understood—by expanding the French *roman à la tasse de thé*—as meaning a realistic piece of fiction in which the heroine serves as chief protagonist, and which can be read with a teacup in one hand without danger of spilling the tea. Mrs. Haywood indeed drew upon her old stock of love scenes tender or importunate, duels, marital disputes, and elopements to lend interest to her story, but except for the mock-marriage with a scoundrelly valet from which the imprudent Betsy is rescued in the nick of time by her former lover, no passage in the four volumes recommends itself particularly either to sense or to sensibility. There are few high lights in "Betsy Thoughtless"; the story keeps the even and loquacious tenor of its way after a fashion called insipid by the "Monthly Review," though the critic finally acknowledges the difficulty of the task, if not the success of the writer. "In justice to (our author), however, this may be further observed, that no other hand would, probably, have more happily finished a work begun on such a plan, as that of the history of a young inconsiderate girl, whose little foibles, without any natural vices of the mind, involve her in difficulties and distresses, which, by correcting, make her wiser, and deservedly happy in the end. A heroine like this, cannot but lay her historian under much disadvantage; for tho' such an example may afford lessons of prudence, yet how can we greatly interest ourselves in the fortune of one, whose character and conduct are neither amiable nor infamous, and which we can neither admire, nor love, nor pity, nor be diverted with? Great spirit in the writer, and uncommon beauties in the expression, are certainly necessary to supply the deficiency of such a barren foundation."[11] Neither of the latter qualities was at the command of the "female pen" that composed "Betsy Thoughtless," but in spite of the handicap imposed by the plan of her work and the deficiencies of her genius, she produced a novel at once realistic and readable. Without resorting to the dramatic but inherently improbable plots by which Richardson made his writings at once "the joy of the chambermaids of all nations"[12] and something of a laughing stock to persons capable of detecting their absurdities, Mrs. Haywood preserved his method of minute fidelity to actual life and still made her book entertaining to such a connoisseur of fiction as Lady Mary Wortley Montagu.[13] Though rarely mentioned with entire approbation, "Betsy Thoughtless" was widely read for fifty years after its publication,[14] and undoubtedly deserves its place among the best of the minor novels collected in Harrison's "Novelist's Library."

In the same useful repertory of eighteenth century fiction is the second of Mrs. Haywood's domestic novels, only less famous than its predecessor. Like her earlier effort, too, "The History of Jemmy and Jenny Jessamy" (1753) contains a great number of letters quoted at full length, though the narrative is usually retarded rather than developed by these effusions. Yet all the letters, together with numerous digressions and inserted narratives, serve only to fill out three volumes in twelves. To readers whose taste for fiction has been cloyed by novels full of incident, movement, and compression, nothing could be more

---

11. *Monthly Review*, V, 393, October, 1751.

12. *Letters from the Lady Mary Wortley Montagu*, Everyman edition, 392.

13. *Letters from the Lady Mary Wortley Montagu*, Everyman edition, 457.

14. *Notes and Queries*, Series VIII, IX, 366. In Smollett's *Ferdinand Count Fathom*, Chap. XXXIX, Captain Miniken recommends as "modern authors that are worth reading" the *Adventures of Loveill, Lady Frail, Bampfylde Moore Carew, Young Scarron*, and *Miss Betsy Thoughtless*. See also A.L. Barbauld, *Correspondence of Samuel Richardson* (1804), IV, 55–6, and the *Autobiography and Correspondence of Mary Granville, Mrs. Delaney* (1861), First series, III, 79, 214.

maddening than the leisurely footpace at which the story drags its slow length along. No wonder, then, that Scott recorded his abhorrence of the "whole Jemmy and Jenny Jessamy tribe," while to Coleridge and Thackeray "Jemmy Jessamy stuff" was a favorite synonym for the emotional inane.[15] But Mrs. Haywood made no pretense of interesting such readers. In the running fire of comment on the narrative contained in the lengthy chapter headings she confesses that her book "treats only on such matters as, it is highly probable, some readers will be apt to say might have been recited in a more laconick manner, if not totally omitted; but as there are others, the author imagines much the greater number, who may be of a different opinion, it is judged proper that the majority should be obliged." She has no hesitation either in recommending parts of the story that "cannot fail of giving an agreeable sensation to every honest and good-natured reader," or in sparing him a "digression of no consequence to the history" which may be "read or omitted at discretion." But those who love to "read in an easy-chair, either soon after dinner, or at night just going to rest," will find in the tale "such things as the author is pretty well convinced, from a long series of observations on the human mind, will afford more pleasure than offence."

We have every reason to believe that what the novelist terms her "distressful narrative" succeeded in its appeal to the Martha Buskbodys of the generation, for even Goethe's Charlotte took a heartfelt interest in the fortunes of Miss Jenny.[16] It was indeed so far calculated to stir the sensibilities that a most touching turn in the lovers' affairs is labeled "not fit to be read by those who have tender hearts or watry eyes." But though popular with sentimental readers, the new production was not wholly approved by the critic of the "Monthly Review."[17] He finds the

---

15. J.G. Lockhart, *Life of Scott*, Everyman edition, 34. Coleridge's *Letters*, I, 368.

16. W. Scott, *Old Mortality*, Conclusion. Goethe's *Werke* (E. Schmidt, Leipsig, 1910), III, 17.

17. That the *Monthly's* review of *Betsy Thoughtless*, complaining of that novel's lack of "those entertaining introductory chapters, and digressive essays, which distinguish the works of a *Fielding*, a *Smollett*, or the author of *Pompey* the little," rankled in the fair novelist's memory is illustrated by a retort in her next work, *Jemmy and Jenny Jessamy*, III, Chap. XVIII, which "contains none of those beautiful digressions, those remarks or reflections, which a certain would-be critick pretends are so much distinguished in the writings of his two favorite authors; yet it is to be hoped, will afford sufficient to please all those who are willing to be pleased." For the review of *Jemmy and Jenny Jessamy*, see *Monthly Review*, VIII, 77.

character and conduct of Miss Jessamy more interesting to the reader than those of Miss Thoughtless, but he does not fail to point out that the fable is equally deficient in plot and in natural incidents. The history, in fact, though it does not want a hero, having like "The Fortunate Foundlings" double the usual number of protagonists, has a more uncommon want, that of a story.

When the novel begins, Jemmy, son of a landed gentleman, and his cousin Jenny, daughter of a wealthy merchant, have long been affianced by their respective parents, but each is left an orphan before their union can be accomplished. Thereupon Jemmy leaves Oxford and comes up to London, where he and Jenny indulge innocently, but with keen relish, in the pleasures of the town.

But the numerous instances of marital levity and unhappiness that come to their notice, make them decide to defer their marriage until they have gained more knowledge of the world and of their own sentiments. In pursuance of this delicate experiment each communicates to the other his observations on the jealousy, discontent, and misery attending marriage. Jenny notes how Mrs. Marlove's partiality for her froward maid promotes discord in the family, and Jemmy is shocked to find the fair Liberia so fond of cards that "though at present a profest enemy to religion, she would be the greatest devotee imaginable, were she once persuaded there were gaming-tables in heaven."

While the two lovers are thus engaged in a pleasant but indecisive daily round of amusement, Bellpine, a false friend, tries to turn Jemmy's affection to the fair musician, Miss Chit, in order to win Jenny for himself, but failing in that, circulates rumors of Jemmy's attachment to Miss Chit in hopes of alienating the lovers' regard. Emboldened by these reports of Jemmy's change of heart, Sir Robert Manley pays his court to Jenny on her way to Bath with her friends Miss Wingman and Lady Speck, but she gently repulses him and will believe nothing to Jemmy's disadvantage. She is saved from the rudeness of Celandine by the intrusion of the gallant's jealous mistress, who faints when foiled in her attempt to stab Jenny, but later relates the story of her ruin. This narrative is enough to disgust Lady Speck with her foppish admirer and to make her sensible of the merits of Mr. Lovegrove. In spite of Bellpine's industrious slander and in spite of seemingly incontrovertible proof of Jemmy's inconstancy, Jenny's faith in her lover remains unshaken. After tedious delays he finally rejoins her in London, but learning the full extent of Bellpine's treachery, he wounds him seriously in a duel and is obliged to seek safety in France. After causing the lovers untold anxiety, the injured man recovers, and Jenny forestalls her lover's return by joining her friends on their wedding journey to Paris. There she finds her adored Jessamy now fully sensible of the merits of his treasure. He does not fail to press for a speedy termination to their delays, and Jenny is not unwilling to crown his love by a "happy catastrophe."

Besides being unwarrantably expanded by a wealth of tedious detail, the novel has little merit as a piece of realism. The society of Lord Humphreys and Lady Specks was not that in which Eliza Haywood commonly moved, but she had lived upon the skirts of gay life long enough to imitate its appearances. Although she exhibits the diamond tassels sparkling in St. James's sun or the musk and amber that perfume the Mall, she never penetrates beyond externalities. The sentiments of her characters are as inflated as those of a Grandison and her picture of refined society as ridiculously stilted as Richardson's own. The scene whether in London, Bath, Oxford, or Paris, is described with more attention to specific detail than appeared in her early romances, but compared with the setting of "Humphrey Clinker" her glittering world appears pale and unreal. Mrs. Haywood had so framed her style to suit the short, rapid tale of passion that she never moved easily in the unwieldy novel form. Consequently her best narrative is to be found in the digressions, a chapter or two long, which are equivalent to little histories upon the old model. In them the progress of the action is unimpeded, compressed, and at times even sprightly.

Recognizing, perhaps, her inability to cope with a plot of any extent, Mrs. Haywood adopted in her next novel a plan that permitted her to include a pot-pourri of short narratives, conversations, letters, reflections, and miscellaneous material without damaging the comprehensive scheme of her story. Except that it lacks the consistent purpose of traducing the fair fame of her contemporaries,[18] "The Invisible Spy" (1755), written under the pseudonym of "Exploralibus," is not essentially different in structure from the "Memoirs of a Certain Island." Love is still the theme of most of the anecdotes, no longer the gross passion that proves every woman at heart a rake, but rather a

---

18. A possible return to scandal-mongering should be noted. *Letters from the Lady Mary Wortley Montagu*, Everyman edition, 461. "You should have given me a key to the Invisible Spy, particularly to the catalogue of books in it. I know not whether the conjugal happiness of the D. of B. (Duke of Bedford) is intended as a compliment or an irony."

romantic tenderness that inclines lovely woman to stoop to folly. From the world of Lady Mellasin, Harriot Loveit, Mr. Trueworth, Lord Huntley, Miss Wingman, and other Georgian fashionables that filled the pages of "Betsy Thoughtless" and "Jemmy and Jenny Jessamy" we are transported again to the pale company of Celadon, Alinda, Placentia, Adario, Melanthe. A framework analogous to that in Le Sage's "Le Diable Boiteux" takes the place of a plot. With a belt of invisibility and a recording tablet, Exploralibus is able to collect whatever is affecting, ludicrous, vicious, or otherwise noteworthy in the conversation, actions, and manners of society. But the shadowy nature of the observer fails to give to the necessarily disconnected incidents even the slight unity possible in the adventures of a lap-dog, a cat, a mouse, a flea, or a guinea. The contents of a single section of "The Invisible Spy" is enough to show how little thought the author expended upon the sequence of the narrative.

Book VI. Disguised as her husband, a villain carries off the young Matilda from a masquerade and ruins her. Alexis sends her away to the country and endeavors to forget her in the pleasures of the town. The contents of a lady's pocket:—a catalogue of imaginary books attributed to the initials of well known persons of quality; two letters, the first from Philetes to excuse his attendance, and the other from Damon making an appointment on the spot where the pocket was found. The foppish Miss Loiter is contrasted with the well trained children of Amadea. Narcissa, endeavoring to avoid marriage with the detested Oakly, is entrapped by the brother of her waiting-maid, who though only a common soldier, poses as Captain Pike.

Though the novel exhibits some pictures of life which at the time were considered natural,[19] and some bits of satire rather extravagant than striking, its appearance was a tacit admission of the failing of the author's powers. Much experience of human nature Mrs. Haywood had undoubtedly salvaged from her sixty years of buffeting about in the world, but so rapid and complete had been the development of prose fiction during her literary life that she was unable quite to comprehend the magnitude of the change. Her early training in romance writing had left too indelible a stamp upon her mind. She was never able to apprehend the full possibilities of the newer fiction, and her success as a novelist was only an evidence of her ability to create the image

---

19. *Gentleman's Magazine*, XXIV, 560, December 1754.

GEORGE WHICHER

of a literary form without mastering its technique. So at the maturity of her powers she lacked a vessel worthy of holding the stores of her experience, and first and last she never exceeded the permutations of sensationalism possible in the short amatory romance.

Long after Mrs. Haywood's death in 1756 came out the last novel presumably of her composing. "The History of Leonora Meadowson," published in two volumes in 1788, is but a recombination of materials already familiar to the reading public. Leonora rashly yields to the wishes of her first lover, weds another, and makes yet a second experiment in matrimony before she finds her true mate in the faithful Fleetwood, whom she had thought inconstant. Thus she is a near relation of the thoughtless Betsy, and possibly a descendant of the much married heroine of "Cleomelia." Another of Mrs. Haywood's earlier fictions, "The Agreeable Caledonian," had previously been used as the basis of a revision entitled "Clementina" (1768). The reviewer of "Leonora" in the "Critical," though aware of the novel's shortcomings, still laments the passing of "the author of Betsy Thoughtless, our first guide in these delusive walks of fiction and fancy."[20]

> "The spirit which dictated Betsy Thoughtless is evaporated; the fire of the author scarcely sparkles. Even two meagre volumes could not be filled, without a little History of Melinda Fairfax;— without the Tale of Cornaro and the Turk,—a tale told twice, in verse and prose,—a tale already often published, and as often read. Alas, poor author! we catch with regret thy parting breath."

20. *Critical Review*, LXV; 236, March 1788.

VIII

Conclusion

Though Eliza Haywood produced nothing which the world has not willingly let die, yet at least the obituary of her works deserves to be recorded in the history of fiction. Of the many kinds of writing attempted by her during the thirty-six years of her literary adventuring none, considered absolutely, is superior to the novels of her last period. "Betsy Thoughtless" contains at once her best developed characters, most extensive plot, and most nearly realistic setting. But before it was sent to press in 1751, Richardson, Fielding, and Sarah Fielding had established themselves in public favor, and Smollett was already known as their peer. Even in company with "David Simple" Eliza Haywood's most notable effort could not hope to shine. The value, then, of what is, all in all, her best work is greatly lessened by the obvious inferiority of her productions to the masterpieces of the age. As a writer of amatory romances and scandal novels, on the contrary, Mrs. Haywood was surpassed by none of her contemporaries. The immense reputation that she acquired in her own day has deservedly vanished, for though her tales undoubtedly helped to frame the novel of manners, they were properly discarded as useless lumber when once the new species of writing had taken tangible form. Perhaps they are chiefly significant to the modern student, not as revealing now and then the first feeble stirrings of realism, but as showing the last throes of sensational extravagance. The very extreme to which writers of the Haywoodian type carried breathless adventure, warm intrigue, and soul-thrilling passion exhausted the possibilities of their method and made progress possible only in a new direction.

On the technical development of the modern novel the *roman à clef* can hardly have exercised a strong influence. Nor can the lampoons in Mrs. Haywood's anthologies of scandal be valued highly as attempts to characterize. To draw a portrait from the life is not to create a character, still less when the lines are distorted by satire. But the caricaturing of fine ladies and gentlemen cannot have been without effect as a corrective to the glittering atmosphere of courtly life that still permeated the pages of the short, debased romances. The characters of the scandal novels were still princes and courtiers, but their exploits were more licentious than the lowest pothouse amours of picaros and their doxies. The chivalrous conventions of the heroic romances had degenerated into the formalities of gallantry, the exalted modesty of romantic heroines had sunk into a fearful regard for shaky reputations, and the picture of genteel life was filled with scenes of fraud, violence, and vice. As the writers of anti-romances in the previous century had found a delicately malicious pleasure in exhibiting characters drawn from humble and rustic life performing the ceremonies and professing the sentiments of a good breeding foreign to their social position, so the scandal-mongering authors like Mrs. Haywood helped to make apparent the hollowness of the aristocratic conventions even as practiced by the aristocracy and the incongruity of applying exalted ideals derived from an outworn system of chivalry to everyday ladies and gentleman of the Georgian age. Undoubtedly the writers of *romans à clef* did not bargain for this effect, for they clung to their princes and court ladies till the last, leaving to more able pens the task of making heroes and heroines out of cobblers and kitchen wenches. But in representing people of quality as the "vilest and silliest part of the nation" Mrs. Haywood and her ilk prepared their readers to welcome characters drawn from their own station in society, and paved the way for that "confounding of all ranks and making a jest of order," which, though deplored by Lady Mary Wortley Montagu,[1] was nevertheless a condition of progress toward realism.

Quite apart from the slight merit of her writings, the very fact of Mrs. Haywood's long career as a woman of letters would entitle her to much consideration. About the middle of the seventeenth century women romancers, like women poets, were elegant triflers, content to add the lustre of wit to their other charms. While Mme de La Fayette was gaining the plaudits of the urbane world for the *délicatesse* of "La Princesse de Clèves" and the eccentric Duchess of Newcastle was employing her genius upon the fantastic, philosophical "Description of a New World, called the Blazing World" (1668), women of another stamp were beginning to write fiction. With the advent of Mme de Villedieu in France and her more celebrated contemporary, Mrs. Behn, in England, literature became a profession whereby women could command a livelihood. The pioneer *romancières* were commonly adventuresses in life as in letters, needy widows like Mrs. Behn, Mme

1. *Letters from the Lady Mary Wortley Montagu*, Everyman edition, 422.

de Gomez, and Mrs. Mary Davys, or cast mistresses like Mme de Villedieu, Mlle de La Force, and Mrs. Manley, who cultivated Minerva when Venus proved unpropitious. But although the divine Astraea won recognition from easy-going John Dryden and approbation from the profligate wits of Charles II's court, her memory was little honored by the coterie about Pope and Swift. When even the lofty ideals and trenchant style of Mary Astell served as a target for the ridicule of Mr. Bickerstaff's friends,[2] it was not remarkable that such authoresses as Mrs. Manley and Mrs. Haywood should be dismissed from notice as infamous scribbling women. [3] Inded the position of women novelists was anything but assured at the beginning of the eighteenth century. They had to support the disfavor and even the malign attacks of established men of letters who scouted the pretensions of the inelegant to literary fame, and following the lead of Boileau, discredited the romance as absurd and unclassical. Moreover, the moral soundness of fictitious fables was questioned by scrupulous readers, and the amatory tales turned out in profusion by most of the female romancers were not calculated to reassure the pious, even though prefaced by assertions of didactic aim and tagged with an exemplary moral. Nevertheless the tribe of women who earned their living chiefly by the proceeds of their pens rapidly increased.[4]

Mrs. Haywood, as we have seen, looked to the booksellers for support when her husband disclaimed her. Of all the amazons of prose fiction who in a long struggle with neglect and disparagement demonstrated the fitness of their sex to follow the novelist's calling, none was more persistent, more adaptable, or more closely identified with the development of the novel than she. Mrs. Behn and Mrs. Manley must be given credit as pioneers in fiction, but much of their best work was written for the stage. Eliza Haywood, on the other hand, added little to her reputation by her few dramatic performances. She achieved her successes first and last as a writer of romances and novels, and unlike

2. *Tatler*, Nos. 32, 59, 63.

3. See also Horace Walpole, *Letters*, edited by Mrs. P. Toynbee, I, 354.

4. Only rarely did women like Mary Astell or Mrs. Elizabeth Rowe become authors to demonstrate a theory or to inculcate principles of piety, and still more seldom did such creditable motives lead to the writing of fiction. Perhaps the only one of the *romancières* not dependent in some measure upon the sale of her works was Mrs. Penelope Aubin, who in the Preface to *Charlotta Du Pont* (dedicated to Mrs. Rowe) declares, "My Design in writing, is to employ my leisure Hours to some Advantage to myself and others. . . I do not write for Bread."

GEORGE WHICHER

Mrs. Aubin and her other rivals continued to maintain her position as a popular author over a considerable period of time. During the thirty-six years of her activity the romances of Defoe and of Mrs. Jane Barker gave place to the novels of Richardson, Fielding, and Smollett, yet the "female veteran" kept abreast of the changes in the taste of her public and even contributed slightly to produce them. Nor was her progress accomplished without numerous difficulties and discouragements. In spite of all, however, Mrs. Haywood remained devoted to her calling and was still scribbling when the great Dr. Johnson crowned the brows of Mrs. Charlotte Lennox to celebrate the publication of "The Life of Harriot Stuart" (1750). After such recognition a career in letters was open to women without reproach. Though unlaureled by any lexicographer, and despised by the virtuous Mrs. Lennox,[5] Mrs. Haywood, nevertheless, had done yeoman service in preparing the way for modest Fanny Burney and quiet Jane Austen. Moreover she was the only one of the old tribe of *romancières* who survived to join the new school of lady novelists, and in her tabloid fiction rather than in the criminal biography, or the *voyage imaginaire*, or the periodical essay, may best be studied the obscure but essential link between the "voluminous extravagances" of the "Parthenissa" kind and the hardly less long-winded histories of "Pamela" and "Clarissa."

5. The salacious landlady in Mrs. Lennox's *Henrietta* tries to discourage the heroine from reading *Joseph Andrews* by recommending Mrs. Haywood's works, ". . . 'there is Mrs. Haywood's Novels, did you ever read them? Oh! they are the finest love-sick, passionate stories; I assure you, you'll like them vastly: pray take a volume of Haywood upon my recommendation.'—'Excuse me,' said Henrietta," etc. *The Novelist's Magazine* (Harrison), XXIII, 14.

A Note About the Author

George Whicher was an American literary scholar and instructor at the University of Illinois. *The Life and Romances of Mrs. Eliza Haywood* (1915), a monograph, was completed as part of his Ph.D. at Columbia University's Department of English and Comparative Literature.

A Note from the Publisher

Spanning many genres, from non-fiction essays to literature classics to children's books and lyric poetry, Mint Edition books showcase the master works of our time in a modern new package. The text is freshly typeset, is clean and easy to read, and features a new note about the author in each volume. Many books also include exclusive new introductory material. Every book boasts a striking new cover, which makes it as appropriate for collecting as it is for gift giving. Mint Edition books are only printed when a reader orders them, so natural resources are not wasted. We're proud that our books are never manufactured in excess and exist only in the exact quantity they need to be read and enjoyed.

Discover more of your favorite classics with Bookfinity™.

- Track your reading with custom book lists.
- Get great book recommendations for your personalized Reader Type.
- Add reviews for your favorite books.
- AND MUCH MORE!

Visit **bookfinity.com** and take the fun Reader Type quiz to get started.

Enjoy our classic and modern companion pairings!